Maddie's Miracles

A Book of Life

SCOTT KRAMER

This book is dedicated to Maddie and Lily, our original Miracles and Lights. And to Pammy, the heart and soul behind Team Maddie.

Prologue

Every parent thinks their child is one in a million. On April 21, 2017, we discovered that Maddie, our two-and-a-half-year-old daughter, really was. Because that's approximately how many children per year are diagnosed with the type of rare, cancerous tumor that found itself embedded into Maddie's spinal cord. To be more precise, about 30 to 50 new cases of Maddie's cancer – Atypical Teratoid/Rhabdoid Tumor – present annually in the United States.

As you'll come to find in this book, and as we confirmed over her 8 plus months of cancer treatment, Maddie was one in a million in a number of ways. But perhaps most importantly, she had a zest for life and an incomparable innocence that allowed her to fight this wretched disease with a dance in her step and a smile on her face.

The chapters that follow were taken from blog and journal entries that were written in real-time. They were written on trains. In hospital beds. From waiting rooms. During sleepless nights. In times of hope. And in times of angst. Together, they track our experience, as thirty-something-year-old parents, watching our daughter get pulled into the eye of a cancer storm. And somehow, someway, keep on dancing and smiling through it all.

What started as an effort to update family and friends on Maddie's condition transformed into a shared emotional experience that motivated us to focus on Maddie's daily miracles in the face of her cancerous foe. The support from our family, friends, colleagues, teachers, doctors, nurses, and even complete strangers was overwhelming. We could not have mustered the strength to stand firmly by Maddie's side without each and every one of you who helped us along the way.

Maddie's Miracles is not just a story of Maddie's miraculous courage (although it certainly is that). It's a story of love. It's a story of life. It's a story of loving life. In both darkness and in light. May we all channel Maddie's journey as we tackle life's challenges.

Team Maddie Forever,

The Kramer Family

PART ONE

The Beginning (4/26/17)

On June 26, 2014, we experienced the single greatest miracle of our life. The birth of our firstborn child, Maddie. (No offense to our younger daughter, Lily. Lily, when you're old enough to read this, it's only because you weren't born yet!) For anyone who has met Maddie in person, you know that we're not just being proud parents when we say she has been a special girl from the start. She is exquisitely *bright* in every sense of the word. Wherever Maddie goes, she brings light, love, and a healthy dose of constant chatter better suited for a teenager trapped inside a toddler's body.

Less than three years later, our little ray of sunshine is going to be faced with a darkness that no person – let alone our sweet little girl – should have to experience. On April 21, 2017, Maddie underwent emergency surgery at the Ann & Robert H. Lurie Children's Hospital of Chicago after an emergency MRI revealed a tumor in her spinal cord. The surgery itself was as successful as we could have hoped. Our doctor was wonderful, and he removed the tumor with a precision that even Grandpa Arnie, a surgical oncologist in his own right, approved.

Our hope is that this successful surgery is just the first of many miracles ahead for Maddie. Subsequent testing confirmed that the tumor was rare, aggressive, and cancerous, and the journey ahead is daunting. Maddie is currently in physical therapy trying to regain strength and movement in her extremities, as well as her ability to stand or walk on her own, which will be followed by a brutal 52-week cancer treatment plan. Her mobility is further limited by a "collar" engulfing her little neck (doctor's words not ours...in a unanimous parental decision, we elected to go with "necklace").

But make no mistake, there is not a toddler in the world better equipped to keep moving forward. With the help of her amazing medical team, and the cast of plastic Disney characters scattered around her hospital room, Maddie keeps on shining. Despite all the hospital stresses, no one can keep that infectious smile off Maddie's face for long.

In some ways, Maddie is secretly loving certain aspects of patient life. She got to sit in a "rocket ship chair" while taking her first ambulance ride, she's watched *Frozen* at least 15 times in full in less than a week (culminating in a hysterical sleep deprivation induced 10:00 p.m. diatribe where she recited about 5 consecutive minutes of *Frozen* dialogue without missing a word), and even Grandma and Gaga can't keep up with Maddie's cookie cravings.

Pammy and I have one mission for Maddie at this point – to keep her as loved, happy, and secure as possible through an otherwise unimaginable experience. We couldn't do that without the love and support of our family and friends. We are beyond blessed to have an unwavering team behind us that ensures we maintain the strength to help Maddie continue to be Maddie. We have been overwhelmed with the outpouring of support – the gift baskets, the toys, the text messages, voicemails, e-mails, and phone calls. Your thoughtfulness is beyond words, and we're just sorry we can't respond individually with an equal amount of love and detail.

Our wish is that our writing will not only document our journey (and give you all the updates surrounding Maddie that we'll be unable to consistently convey individually), but also serve as a ray of hope for us to rally around. Pammy and I know that Maddie has just begun to deliver more miracles. And for now, we are going to cherish those miracles, no matter how big or small, one day at a time.

Rise Up (4/27/17)

On April 20, 2017, the night we brought Maddie to the emergency room, we had thought she just had a nasty virus. She had been experiencing pain in her neck for the previous seven days, which we believed stemmed from swollen lymph nodes in the area. This diagnosis was confirmed by three previous doctor visits. The only reason we even went to the emergency room that night was that Maddie started to get rashes on her hands. Our pediatrician thought, out of an abundance of caution, we should have her examined in order to rule out "Kawasaki Disease," an unlikely condition associated with hand rashes and neck pain. As we walked through the ER doors, with the sun setting in the background, we had no idea of the darkness that awaited inside.

Upon arrival, Maddie and I sat in the waiting room together. We watched *Lion Guard*, ate animal crackers, and drank apple juice. A regular ole Daddy/Maddie date night. My biggest worry was the emergency room copay.

The nurse then called us into triage. She asked me to place Maddie on the scale. I excitedly started to put Maddie down and playfully chit chat with her about how much we thought she would weigh.

Then it happened.

As I set Maddie on the scale, both of her little legs went limp. She couldn't bear any weight whatsoever. I could feel my heart stop as I watched her crumble. The same sweet girl whose main weakness in life was her inability to sit still for more than five seconds was dependent on me to carry her back to the waiting room.

My voice shaking in fear, I asked the nurse my quivering question. "That's probably just atrophy, right? She's been laying around a lot the last few days." I saw the intense look of concern on her face as she tried to calmly tell me that my theory was possible.

Over the course of the evening, Maddie started to progressively lose movement on her left side. Her left arm and left leg were largely immobile. Despite multiple attempts in front of doctors and nurses, she didn't show any ability to walk the rest of the evening. Numerous painful physical exams and countless hours later, the MRI results came back sometime past midnight on April 21st.

As the Neurology Fellow knelt before Pammy and me in the waiting room, she wrapped her hands around her neck. Before she even started speaking, as she struggled to mouth a single sound, we already knew. We didn't hear the exact explanation that would eventually follow. But her body language said more than words could convey. My atrophy theory was out the window.

Maddie had her emergency surgery that morning. The wait was agonizing. I'll spare you the devastating detail for another day. But needless to say, the fear and pain of sitting in a waiting room – while your precious baby girl is undergoing surgery to save her life – without any guarantees of who is going to emerge (let alone *if* she will emerge) is a hell that no human should ever experience.

But by some miracle, our little Maddie emerged. She appeared every bit herself mentally and emotionally. Only her physical abilities were left hanging in the immediate balance, as the left side of her body remained immobile, and we had not seen her stand on her own, let alone walk, for more than a week.

And so six days after hospital admission (as I slowly regain my ability to breathe, speak, or type anything meaningful beyond tears), we're now at the Shirley Ryan AbilityLab rehabilitation center in Chicago. Our first order of business — get little Maddie back on her feet and hopefully regain strength and mobility before the cancer treatment begins.

We had our first physical therapy session this morning. With her world recently rocked, Maddie spent the entire session refusing to play. She wasn't going to perform for anyone. Let alone Mike from AbilityLab. Pammy and I talked about whether this place could make an impact on her if she wasn't going to play by the rules.

But then, two hours later, Maddie unveiled another miracle. With the support of nothing but Grandma's iPad, Maddie stood on her own two feet. Our second miracle in six days. Survival. Then Standing. One miracle at a time.

Maddie likely has weeks of physical therapy ahead of her, but seeing this type of miraculous progress was an incredible start. You can only keep Maddie down for so long before she rises back up. Watch out, Mike from AbilityLab. Maddie's coming for you!

Walking on Sunshine (4/28/17)

Two days ago, the manager at the rehabilitation center pulled me aside and asked, "What are your goals for Maddie's time at AbilityLab?" It struck me as an odd question. Does this person realize that I just spent more than 36 gut-wrenching hours not knowing whether I was ever going to speak to Maddie again? And she's going to ask me about goals for physical rehabilitation?

Talk about perspective. I could never imagine viewing Maddie's ability to walk as inconsequential. But from the time Maddie went into the operating room to the time we entered AbilityLab, I didn't spend one second thinking about whether Maddie's legs would return to full function. I prayed for just one thing – to be able to talk to Maddie again as that pure, happy child that she has always been. It didn't matter to me what physical body stored that happiness. I just wanted her to be *herself*, in all her smiling/silly/happy glory.

Oddly enough, unbeknownst to me, Pammy was asked the same question in a separate meeting that same day. And both of our answers were identical. Putting aside that we're currently in a place specializing in physical rehabilitation, our primary concern is keeping Maddie as Maddie. Allowing her to keep on finding joy in her family, her friends, and her television shows and characters as opposed to letting the poking, prodding, and isolation break her psyche.

So far, with the support of our families, we're achieving our goal. Maddie spent the majority of today laughing, smiling, playing games, and just being Maddie.

Although Pammy and I may not have had a physical agenda for AbilityLab, Maddie had other plans. Seven days removed from her surgery, Maddie blew away the entire staff today by taking her first independent steps down the "yellow brick road" with none other than her therapist, Sofia (certainly some distant relation to *Sofia the First*). She built on these early morning steps with even more monitored walking in her second therapy session with Jordan (who may or may not have confused Maddie's rehab as her training for the Toddler Navy SEALs). By the end of the evening, Maddie was confidently strutting her stuff down the hallway – restrictive necklace and all – showing off to her Aunt Jamie. With this unbelievably quick advancement, Jordan let us know that she may have to go back to the drawing board with Maddie, as Maddie had already exceeded the goals Jordan had set for Maddie for the duration of her entire time at AbilityLab. Goals she had created only *one day earlier.*

While Maddie still has miles to go in her physical rehabilitation, it's amazing to see her confidence grow. For Pammy and me, her walking is just icing on the cake. We both understand that the long journey through cancer treatment begins very shortly. And that keeping Maddie feeling loved, happy, and confident will be the best rehabilitation that AbilityLab can provide.

Don't tell Maddie that though. She's planning on racing her Daddy down the hallways tomorrow.

Riding My Tricycle Feeling So Free (4/29/17)

One of Maddie's most special traits has always been her knack for greeting people with love. Her infectious, smiling welcome is irresistible. When approaching strangers, Maddie has a tendency to break the ice a bit. Rather than dip her toes in the social waters with a simple hello, she dives right in with one of these beauties: "I saw Olaf today!" Or more recently, "I'm a big sister!" No need to dispense with canned pleasantries, let's kick this conversation off with what matters!

Over the course of her hospital stay, Pammy and I saw the challenges of inpatient life start chipping away at Maddie's infectious greetings. When nurse after nurse and doctor after doctor comes in to draw blood, futz with your I.V., or God forbid – as we've come to realize – take your blood pressure with an automated, tourniquet-style device (what happened to the good old fashioned manual hand pump???), it gets hard to chit chat about Olaf or sisterhood. Instead, Maddie fell into replacing her ice breakers with her newfound icy fears. "Don't touch me!" Or, "Daddy, can you talk to the doctor outside?" Or my personal favorite as the new nurse arrives for the next shift expecting to find a happy-go-lucky little toddler: "Can you go home?" If anyone comes too close to Maddie's shrinking radius of physical security, cue the hysterics.

Thankfully, Maddie's time at AbilityLab has this little social butterfly spreading her chatty wings again. Free from the fears of needles and nurses, Maddie spent her two hours of physical therapy today playing with her therapists like they had known each other for years. Surrounded by family members eagerly watching her every move for improvement in gross motor skills, Maddie remained immersed in her imaginary world of Disney and Peppa Pig characters and smiled her way through each session. By far, today was Maddie's best day of smiles and socialization. So much so that one of her therapists asked if she was available tomorrow to take some pictures for the marketing department (and to my surprise, it was not because their new motto is going to be: "AbilityLab – Can you go home?").

As her social confidence soars, so too does her physical growth. After taking those first independent steps yesterday, Maddie took to the road today on a sweet lime green tricycle. With her Aunt Mimi and Aunt Risa rooting from the sidelines, Maddie cruised her Green Hog right out of the rehab room through the hallways. You would've thought an army of angry needle toting nurses were chasing her from behind. But nope. Maddie's wheels were moving on the heels of confidence and thrills. She was entirely free from fear. She was just Maddie.

And we can't wait to hear what comes out of Maddie's mouth tomorrow morning when the first shift arrives to say hello.

You've Got a Friend in Me (4/30/17)

After putting Maddie down for bed tonight, I quietly slipped into the AbilityLab bathroom to wash up. With the door cracked, I could hear her singing softly. It was the chorus from Randy Newman's *You've Got a Friend in Me*. After hours of watching *Frozen* and *Finding Dory* from her hospital bed, she unexpectedly pulled out this classic song from *Toy Story*.

I'd like to think Maddie didn't choose this song by accident. Because for the first time post-surgery, Maddie was blessed to return to the normalcy of just being with friends. There are no therapy sessions on Sunday. No fine motor musings. No supervised playtime. Just time to be a kid. And boy did she ever take advantage.

After spending a great morning with Aunts Risa and Mimi, and a surprise visit from our good friends, Sam and Jesse (who Maddie still thinks must know Woody and Buzz on account of his name), Maddie's special, toddler friend Winnie came by to play to cap off the evening. It was pure magic.

To Maddie's surprise, Winnie brought a friend all the way from Arendelle – Queen Elsa herself (or at least Waukegan, Illinois' finest stand-in). Maddie was in awe. She couldn't wait to tell Elsa all about her new toys and fill her in on what goes on outside of Arendelle and inside places like Daniel Tiger's neighborhood.

Apparently, the feeling was mutual. Because Elsa – on her own accord – ended up staying through dinner after probably only allotting time for a quick visit. She was enamored by Maddie. Although it probably didn't hurt that Maddie's Uncle B and Aunt Mary brought in Smoque BBQ for dinner tonight. How often does Elsa get a chance to lay off the ice pops and just have a little brisket?

As the night concluded, all Maddie wanted to do was walk down the hallway with her buddy, Winnie. No parents allowed. Just friends. We followed closely behind, and their interaction was soul-warming. They held hands their entire walk. Maddie stopped to compliment Winnie on everything from her shirt, to her hair, to her "beautiful heart." They hugged more times than I can remember. And apparently, when Winnie got home, her dad asked her, "What did you tell Maddie today?" Her response? "I love you with all my heart."

And we love you too, Winnie. You've got a friend in Maddie.

The Magic of an Uneventful Day (5/1/17)

Ever since we had kids, I've had a perpetual case of *shpilkes* on the weekends or other days off work. For our non-Yiddish speaking readers (and those who didn't otherwise pick up the vernacular from Linda Richman on *Saturday Night Live*), this basically means I can't sit still for a minute. As Pammy knows all too well, Saturday morning hits and my inner toddler screams for activity. Gone was the uneventful, "relaxing" day around the house. Once the baby monitor (otherwise known as a parent's alarm) told us it was morning, I was ready to roll. Let's go to the zoo, try a new restaurant, walk to a nearby park, or hit the beach for those two months out of the year where you don't need a parka to live here (that's an exaggeration for our East Coast family who still somehow believe they live in the tropics compared to Chicago). But God forbid, please let's not just sit around our home and have an uneventful day. What could be more anxiety-inducing than sitting still when we have a whole day free to roam?

What a difference a week makes. Today, our sweet Maddie experienced an uneventful day. And it couldn't have been more beautiful. No medical updates. No nurse drama. No page turning milestones. Maddie just spent a relaxing day in her "new room" (her words not mine) at AbilityLab and played with her therapists like she was in our playroom at home. Uneventful never felt so good.

Maddie's return to normalcy continued when her nanny and best friend, Day, joined Gaga, Pop Pop, Aunt Jennifer, and me for a dinner filled with chicken fingers and giggles. For a brief moment, Maddie's infectious laughs and playful interactions made me forget where we were. With my eyes and ears focused on Maddie, it was just a normal dinner with our smiling girl.

As Maddie's night came to an end, a volunteer magician slipped into our room. She taught Maddie a few tricks and confirmed for Maddie what we all already know – there are more than a few special powers packed into this literal diaper dandy!

But the real magic came well before our amateur Houdini's slights of hand. Even this shpilkinating daddy was spellbound by the magic of our first uneventful day since this all-too-eventful-show began. I can only pray for more uneventful moments to come. Let's hope there's a more powerful magician out there making that trick possible.

The Force (5/2/17)

Maddie slept last night from 8:30 p.m. to 6:30 a.m. largely without interruption in her AbilityLab crib. You'd think that block of rest would be a welcome reprieve for Daddy as well. But while I was thrilled for Maddie, the quiet time tends to be the most difficult time for me. During Maddie's awake hours, I am laser focused on just being present with her. I don't have the time, capacity, or energy to enter into the empty space of a worrying mind. But when I'm through chasing Maddie around the halls in awe of her miraculous physical recovery, when her giggles fade into restful breaths...the mind tends to wander. Well, the adult mind tends to wander.

Maddie is a different bird. Maddie woke up cheerful as can be at 6:30 a.m. "Daddy, we need to go to the store and get a Grandpere," she said, referring to one of the few plush *Daniel Tiger's Neighborhood* characters she has yet to receive in the overwhelming support of amazing hospital gifts. "Daddy, we also need to go to the store and get Buzz Lightyear." Because what kid could possibly have a Woody without a Buzz.

Maddie is just over a week removed from emergency surgery to remove a cancerous tumor from her spinal cord. The images of breathing tubes, NG tubes, and who knows what else protruding from that adorable face still haunt me. I can feel my throat tightening at the thought of her legs going limp in triage. She hasn't slept in her own bed in 12 days. And yet her #1 concern for this fine Tuesday morning? Topping off her character collection of course! If that's not childhood at its finest, I don't know what is.

Maddie has taught me so much already about the power of staying in the present. To the point where I wonder if these astounding medical recoveries we hear about in children have anything to do with their ever-present state of mind. Unlike her adult caretakers, who can't help but burden themselves with the creeping thoughts of the future. The what-ifs. The what-once-was. The what-could-be. Maddie is truly just living in the moment.

To Maddie, she is no longer in a rehab center. This is Maddie Kramer's Neighborhood and everyone else is just along for the trolley ride. You should see her walk down these halls now. "Hi Eugene!" she calls to the 6'5" dreadlocked man delivering her food. "Hello Yessie!" she yells to a member of the nursing staff. She's walking, waving, and greeting employees with the kindness of a cordial co-worker.

Her confidence is just soaring generally as well. We knew Maddie had reached the apex when she finally went toe-to-toe with her enemy. The dreaded "V" word. *Vitals.* Since leaving Lurie, nothing struck fear into Maddie like taking her pulse, her temperature, or last but not least, the evil blood pressure. Not today, nemesis. Maddie walks up to the Vitals Machine. She tracks down one of her favorite nurses, Gigi. Maddie brings her over to the Vitals Machine and says, "Gigi, can we do this?" Maddie sticks out her finger, as if accepting her fate, to start step one: the pulse. Without tears, she then finishes off the remaining process – temperature, check; blood pressure, check. Take that, Darth Vitals.

And that wasn't quite enough for Maddie. She was going for the gusto. Maddie stands in front of the now defeated Darth Vitals and chit chats about her future. She says that maybe she'll be a doctor one day. And then goes on to explore other newfound possibilities in the post Darth Vitals World, "If I can be a cook. Or a writer..." Never mind that Pammy and I quickly realized that she was just reciting verbatim a line from one of her favorite Sesame Street books, she had just defeated Darth Vitals and she was on to her Episode II. One Vitals Machine down, Maddie makes her way triumphantly to the second machine. No messing around this time. Without flinching, Maddie reaches in and grabs one of the inner parts of the machine as if to claim her own version of a scalp to memorialize her victory.

It was a thing of beauty. Dream on, Maddie Kramer. Your force could not be stronger.

Let it Go (5/3/17)

It's Friday morning at 7:30 a.m. on April 21st. Pammy and I have been awake for more than 24 hours. All we know at this point is that the MRI did not look good, and that we had witnessed Maddie's body start to crumble before our eyes. We had been told that the neurosurgery team would arrive shortly with a surgical plan. We hadn't yet met any of the team members. And we had no pregame previews of the Xs and Os of the plan.

When the clock hits 7:30 a.m., we see an army of doctors marching down the hall. This must be the team. The quarterback and lead surgeon, Dr. Alden, asks us to huddle in a small nook behind the nurse's station. Only there's no fourth quarter, motivational speech waiting for us. Instead, he pops on the computer and shows us a black and white image with the outline of a small head, a toddler body, and a spine running vertically down the screen. No curly hair. No adorable smile. No beautiful long eyelashes. Our bright, colorful girl is reduced to the black and white MRI outline with a grey-like blob floating in her spinal cord.

Dr. Alden describes the surgical plan without even breaking for air. I only hear numbers. The tumor covers 4 levels of her spine. Surgery will be somewhere between 4-6 hours. She'll be in the hospital for 2 weeks. She'll then move to an inpatient physical rehab center for anywhere from 8 weeks to 8 months. She'll wear a collar for at least 6 weeks.

He has a quick case starting in an hour, but then he'll start Maddie's surgery in 2-3 hours.

I don't suppose I can go to the booth for a review right now? At least maybe a 20 second timeout?

Pammy and I understand very quickly that there are no audibles in this playbook. We say our prayers. We cry the last remaining tears left in our bodies. And we wait.

Fast forward to today. Thankfully, the oddsmakers were off on these initial spreads. Hospital for 2 weeks? Try 6 nights. Inpatient rehab for anywhere from 8 weeks to 8 months? Let's go with 8 nights. You heard me. Eight. Nights. We're talking a miracle of biblical proportions here. Or at least Arendelle sized proportions.

That's right – after arriving at AbilityLab entirely unable to walk, Maddie is now going home tomorrow morning on the strength of her own two feet. And with good reason. You should've seen her tonight. She was breathtaking.

Maddie's cousin, Taylor, came by for a pizza party and playtime. I'm pretty sure anyone watching would've thought that Maddie's entire stay was a hoax. Some elaborate scheme for free housing and the enormous cafeteria. Here this little girl was, not just walking down the halls. But moving through a list of verbs that I had assumed were going to be just part of our past tense vocabulary. Running. Jumping. Dancing. Balancing. Climbing.

Maddie, you know they already told you that you get to go home, kid? Nothing left to prove here.

Sweetly, Maddie and Taylor did take about four whole minutes during their evening of activity to just sit and read a book with Aunt Ali (a world record in toddler time). Their focus faded quickly, however, and they turned to what these two do best: make believe. After a few mediocre attempts to re-enact some opening scenes from *Frozen*, this nugget of beauty emerges and concludes their interaction:

Taylor turns to Maddie and asks, "Do you have your magic powers back?"

Maddie doesn't waste a minute in her response. "Yes!"

Let the cancer storm rage on, Maddie. Its icy cold never bothered you anyway.

An Ode to Mommy (5/4/17)

Happy Birthday, Mommy. Not exactly the way we drew this one up. But painfully knowing that we can't change the challenge that has been thrown our way, what better gift could you have than returning home today with our sweet Maddie.

Today, on your birthday, you'll once again sit in the rocking chair in her pink room and calm her to sleep with the soothing sounds of the *Shema* and *Up on the Roof.* You'll read Maddie stories with her snuggled on your lap, as she softly negotiates for "just one more Paddington." And you'll kiss that cool, sweet *keppy* while you lay her into the comfort of that cozy crib.

Make no mistake, our sweet Maddie is who she is because of you. Being a superhero doesn't just happen by accident. And I have no doubt Maddie received her super powers from you. Because you're not just mom. You're Mommy. You're head chef (or, *balabusta* as your mom would say). You're the general manager of Team Cookie Doughs. You're a finance manager. You're a best friend. You're a devoted wife. And you're the love of my life. And more amazingly, somehow, you manage to reserve enough energy to give each and every one of these roles 100% day in and day out.

I can't do what you do. But I can stand in awe of every moment. Watching you grow into the mother you've become has been almost as breathtaking as watching Maddie tackle the early stages of this enormous undertaking. Maddie may be our miracle. But you are my miracle.

I love you, Pammy. Thank you for being you. And for giving Maddie the tools to keep her miracles coming.

Homecoming Reflections (5/4/17)

Since Maddie was born, we've always listened to music in the car. Public service announcement for future parents: Beware of your song choice! Pammy and I thought we were just being fun parents by playing nothing but Disney songs and the free PJ Library CDs (which are basically toddlered down versions of Jewish camp songs) every time we went for a drive. That's what you call a Rookie Mistake.

Fast forward three years, we are now officially prisoners of Maddie's cheesy music war. The moment we set foot in the car, Maddie asks, "Daddy, can we turn on Mickey Songs?" "Daddy, I want to listen to Disney songs." "No Daddy, let's do Shabbat songs." Every now and then, I try to turn on an actual radio station and sing along in a fun, sing-songy voice, hoping to trick her into appreciating a song that has non-animated voices. No such luck. Maddie can spot a human voice a mile away. My lose-lose decision? Mickey Sings or Toddler Screams? I choose Mickey and continue to perpetuate our Partridge Family Predicament. Sure, Maddie's uncanny ability to sing verbatim any Disney movie song from the last 15 years is now just one of her many toddler party tricks. But at what cost?

That brings us to today. After sleeping in hospital beds for more than two weeks, all I want to do is roll the windows down and blast *Born to Run, Learning to Fly,* or some other inspirational rock anthem to carry us home on Maddie's Independence Day. But I know better than to even try. Curiously, Maddie spared us the pleasure of playing perennial fan favorite, *Mousekabunga* by Pete from *Mickey Mouse Clubhouse* (in doing so, she also spared Pammy from having to listen to me imitate Pete's voice for the next 24 hours in the impossible effort to purge the song from my mind).

Bucking all car ride trends, Maddie doesn't ask for any music as we leave AbilityLab. After sitting quietly in her car seat for the first 5 minutes of the drive, she breaks into this tune from *Barney & Friends* as we cruise down Lake Shore Drive...

"If all the raindrops were lemon drops and gum drops..."

If she only knew the sheer power of that line at that moment. Over the past few weeks, we've had our share of raindrops. More like tsunami waves battering our souls. But Pammy and I have done our best to turn our own personal raindrops into lemon drops and gum drops. Or more precisely, taking these tsunami waves of pain and directing them into our own force of nature of love and emotional endurance.

As we left AbilityLab this morning, however, I think we were all left with a mixed bag of emotions. I was unexpectedly first hit with a terrible outpouring of sadness. Not for Maddie. But for many of the other children we met on the floor. There are about 30 rooms on the pediatric-focused 18th floor. While there is no doubt that the storm these last couple of weeks battered our family to the core, we have been blessed with a beautiful ray of sunshine – it's called Hope. Maddie is exceeding all expectations to date. We're able to share smiles, laughs, and songs with our family and friends. We're able to dream of a brighter tomorrow despite the arduous path ahead.

Unfortunately, the other 29 rooms don't all have the hope of sunshine in the forecast. The torrential downpour hitting their families is destined to be ever-present. Permanent breathing machines. Total paralysis. Utter lack of cognition or communication. And the poor parents, many of whom I chatted with over meals or hallway walks, have nothing left to do but endure the storm.

Until that moment, I hadn't really been able to look past our own personal situation. I tuned out the news, the outside world, and certainly other families' problems. On an even broader level, for most of us, we have the luxury of living under our own waterproof umbrellas where tragedies are the things that the news or other less fortunate families are made of. Undoubtedly that was me and Pammy before all of this happened. But Cancer ripped away our umbrella. Not only are we standing outside in the rain, but without the umbrella obstructing our view, we see that there are others enduring an even graver storm by our side.

And so while there is no minimizing the horror of what our family is experiencing, I couldn't also help but leave AbilityLab feeling grateful. It's a crazy thing to say. We're in the eye of this storm, and yet the appreciation is palpable. I feel blessed to have unparalleled support from family and friends. I feel blessed to be in the hands of such phenomenal medical professionals. I feel blessed to have the luxury of leaving AbilityLab where so many others will remain unimproved. And I feel blessed for being able to call myself "Daddy" to the single most amazing little girl I have ever laid eyes on.

I know this is only the beginning, Maddie. But I couldn't be prouder of you. You are the sunshine that follows the rain. You are the light that leads us all through the darkness. You are our umbrella. And we love you.

It is with that feeling of appreciation that we pulled our car up to the home Maddie hadn't seen since April 20th. And yes, by this point, we were serenaded by – surprise,

surprise – yet another Disney singalong (nothing symbolic or poetic to report about the *Tangled* song feeding our animated voice addiction on arrival).

The homecoming could not have been sweeter. Maddie was greeted with a special visit from her older cousins from New Jersey (Sam, Molly, and Zoe). She hugged her two-month-old sister, Lily, tighter than the dreaded blood pressure band wrapped around her leg daily. And as the sun went down this evening, Pammy read Maddie her two bedtime books (somehow staving off the negotiation to read three or four), and I got to sing our sweet girl to sleep and lay her down in a crib that didn't come attached to a nurse's button. And like the perfect ending to this stormy chapter, Maddie went to sleep easily right at her usual bedtime. She was home.

Sweet dreams, Maddie Ila. May your raindrops continue to be lemon drops and gum drops.

L'dor Va'dor (5/5/17)

About 34 years and 9 months ago today, two other parents were experiencing the same sense of intense pain that Pammy and I experienced two weekends ago. Prior to August 2, 1982, they were filled with equal parts excitement and anxiety as their first child was set to arrive.

We parents know that feeling all too well. That feeling when you know that your life is about to get flipped upside down in the most beautiful way imaginable. You just don't know exactly when or how. And for every first-time parent (and frankly, any parent-to-be), every now and then your mind wanders on the teeter-totter of praying for a healthy child and fearing the possibilities of what could go wrong.

For most of us, thankfully, those fears do not become reality. We get to experience the ultimate miracle of life with an unrivaled joy. I can still vividly remember the moment Maddie was born. As Dr. Bonner held her up in the sky in our own personal re-enactment of *The Lion King*, I stared into Maddie's eyes and experienced something out of a sci-fi movie. I felt like I was looking at an earlier version of myself. She just had this unmistakable resemblance that placed me front and center with the Circle of Life. It was a miracle.

Unfortunately, 34 plus years ago, any such miracle for my parents was short-lived. I arrived a little over 4 weeks early. And my body made that very clear to everyone. Sparing you all of the details (mostly because the darkest of those are locked away in my parents' emotional vault), I do know that my stomach was not yet fully closed. I arrived with my intestines literally outside of my body, as the doctors worked to repackage the gift that my parents were long awaiting. Their blessing was not that I was born, but that I survived.

And my blessing? That one of the people watching over me was my mom. The Original Pam Kramer, as my brother-in-law aka Uncle Mikey Boy likes to say.

For those of you who don't know my mom, her greatest strength is her greatest weakness. She is The Ultimate Giver. My mom gives every piece of her mind and body to doing what she can to help other people in times of need or normalcy. It's her beast and her burden. I'm pretty sure my mom spends more time worrying about what she can do to help, or what she didn't do to help, than any other daily activity. She is an unparalleled source of love.

I, for one, can certainly say that I would not be here without that life source. Or I at least would not be the person I am today. Despite a litany of my own medical problems, I am not defined or limited by any of them. This is not something I think about, really ever, but I have no doubt for the maternal reason behind my ability to expunge those pieces of history from who I am.

In September 2001, my parents had to yet again face the darkness that comes with child illness. On the eve of my sister's Bat Mitzvah (a fact that Jennifer will never let any of us forget...sorry again, Jen), I had emergency surgery on my small intestines that ultimately left me hospitalized for more than a month and unenrolled from college for a semester.

And yet for all the emotional and physical difficulty that stretch of time brought, here's what I remember: that my mom spent each and every night sleeping next to me on the dreadfully uncomfortable bench otherwise known as a hospital guest bed. Never mind that I was 19 years old at the time and by all other accounts functional. Never mind that she had three other children at home needing her just as much as I did. She was there for me during the silent hours of the night. The time of thoughts that creep. The time of fears. And she navigated me through the darkness.

Mom, your unending willingness to be there for me – and frankly, for everyone – is your super power. My only prayer is that at least some of that gene dripped into my pool and gives me the strength to see Maddie through the journey that lies ahead for her. But one thing I know for sure. It doesn't matter whether I personally have an ounce of that power or endless gallons. Because I know you'll be there for me. Giving me the support that I need to give every drop within my body to Maddie.

L'dor Va'dor at its finest. Happy Birthday, Mom. (Yes, for those reading closely, my mom Pam Kramer was born on May 5th, and my wife Pammy Kramer was born on May 4th, albeit decades apart. We meet again, Circle of Life.)

The Promise of a New Day (5/6/17)

"Daaaaadddy...come geeeeeet meeeeee."

Every morning, this is the sweet sound I hear from Maddie's voice across our baby monitor. Sometimes it's at 5:00 a.m. Sometimes at 6:30 a.m. The times may vary but the sound remains constant – she whispers the phrase in her typical sing-songy way. If it weren't for the monitor volume turned up, I might not even hear it.

That serenading, sweet sound is my daily restart. No matter what happened the day before, no matter what morning meandering my mind has begun, the moment Maddie's whispers begin, I can't help but smile and think about how lucky I am to have such a special little girl.

What a blessing to feel that sense of refresh every morning. Thich Nhat Hanh, a writer who focuses on the importance of mindfulness and presence in daily living, speaks about mindfulness reminders. He goes as far as to recommend a mindfulness "bell" that rings every so often to remind you to leave the wandering rumination of your mind and focus again on the present moment. To stop the destructive mental gymnastics of the what-ifs, the what-was, and the what-could-be. Maddie has been my own personal mindfulness bell.

One of the most sad and frightening parts of the weeks leading up to Maddie's hospital admission was when our mindfulness bell disappeared. Every morning, for one week straight, she woke up not with her musical whisper, but instead with a primordial scream as she writhed in pain. I cringe just thinking about it. Believing she just had a strained neck from her swollen lymph nodes, I woke up every morning before Maddie and stared at the monitor with bated breath. I would pray that her first words would again be "Daaaaadddy...come geeeeet meeeeee." During the latter few days, I even found myself talking to the monitor. "Come on, Maddie. You can do it." Knowing that if I heard that sweet voice again, it would mean everything was OK. Unfortunately, my prayers were not answered. And one week later we learned why.

Come yesterday morning, Maddie woke up in her own bed for the first time since this all transpired. And wouldn't you know, this was no hospital wake up. I didn't wake up to an alarm clock. I didn't wake up startled by a nightmare. No cries. No screams. Just my favorite sound in the world.

"Daaaaadddy...come geeeeet meeeeee."

Pause. Deep breath. Restart.

What a miraculous way to start a morning.

It's not often that we take the opportunity to restart our minds. Most of us reserve that moment for the weekend or perhaps even a vacation. Thanks to Maddie, I'm able to at least try and restart, try and refocus, every single morning. If only for a moment. Her sweet voice reminds me of what matters in life and reminds me of all the things for which I am thankful.

In some ways, this week at home is our family's opportunity for a more fundamental re-centering before the next big battle. Time to sharpen our mental and emotional knives. Time to give thanks for the gift of a peaceful pause at home. Time for rest. Time for love. And time for prayer.

I don't really know what to expect during the year ahead. Nor do I really want to know. But I pray, that amidst the challenge, we are all afforded pauses of peace. Moments to re-center. And God willing, more mornings beginning with my favorite sound.

"Daaaaadddy...come geeeeeet meeeeee."

See you tomorrow, sweet girl.

Running on Faith (5/7/17)

In the first 48 hours after learning about Maddie's diagnosis, I was utterly broken. Psychologically. Emotionally. Physically. Broken. I couldn't so much as start to talk to, let alone see, even the closest of family or friends without crumbling. I vividly remember leaving the ICU on Day 2 or 3 to force myself to come home, say hi to Lily, and shower before heading back to the painful halls of Lurie Children's Hospital.

I opened the door to our home. I saw two-month-old Lily sleeping sweetly in her mamaRoo. I went to sit down beside her in hopes of finding a moment of reprieve. And I instead curled up into the fetal position and began crying convulsively. The hurt was all-consuming.

After gathering myself, I tried to make my way up the stairs to shower. As I got to the top of the stairs, I didn't realize how intensely the emotional, magnetic force of Maddie's beautifully pink bedroom would pierce my heart. I couldn't get myself to walk past her room into my bedroom to shower. The pain remained too great.

At the time, I remember telling a few people that I could not see my life returning. I could not envision how to make life work again. How to make me work again. My single greatest source of joy, Maddie, was being pulled into a darkness I couldn't have feared in my wildest of nightmares. How could I possibly ever see light?

As I'm sure is common for anyone experiencing such an earth-shattering tragedy, I thought deeply about faith. And God. And fate. The natural, expected questions – how can there be a God if God would allow this to happen? What type of divinity strikes down upon such a perfect little girl? Take me. Take me in the worst, most painful way. But Maddie? Religion be damned.

But I didn't dwell there too long. There is so much suffering in the world. If faith couldn't co-exist with suffering, atheism would've emerged victorious eons ago. What I instead began to appreciate was that, while I was tempted to blame faith for my pain, I was otherwise bestowed a bevy of unparalleled support. How could I curse for the curses but not also be grateful for goodness?

Grateful to live just a short drive from one of the best children's hospitals in the world. Grateful to have a surgeon on call that day named Dr. Alden (who I now otherwise refer to as Superman when he's in his superhero scrubs, and Clark Kent when in his alter ego mode). Grateful to have friends, colleagues, and neighbors who have rallied behind us in the most unimaginably supportive ways. Grateful to have the most dedicated family members, who have dropped everything in their own personal lives to be our first line of defense.

I may want to curse the notion of a higher power for putting us in this nightmare, but I have the utmost faith in the support we have to wake back up again. Who to credit for that faith is almost irrelevant. But because of our outside support, I am able to have faith. That alone is a blessing.

Just a few short weeks ago, I didn't see my life working again. I didn't see myself waking from the nightmare. And yet tomorrow, I am going back to work with my previously battered eyes wide open. Back to support the colleagues who have unabashedly supported me. Back to making my life work again in some capacity.

Make no mistake, our collective recovery is still in its formative stages. And it's inextricably linked to Maddie's progress, which to date has been nothing short of miraculous. But none of this would be possible without you all.

Thank you for your support. Your prayers. Your voicemails. Your text messages. Your gifts. And your various other forms of love. We are forever grateful. As I return to work, my hope is to still be able to write. It just may not be as often. But for all of our sakes, I hope that you continue to receive uplifting updates on Maddie's ongoing miracles. Because Miracle Maddie has only just begun to defy and inspire. My faith in Maddie is limitless.

The Irony of Love (5/8/17)

"Daddy, what day is today?"

"Monday."

"Who's coming today?"

"Gaga and Pop Pop."

"And what are we doing today?"

"We're going to play and maybe go to the zoo."

"Yayyyyyyy!"

Welcome to my morning chats with Maddie. After my favorite wake up alarm, "Daaaaadddy...come geeeeeet meeeeee," we make our way into Mommy and Daddy's bed, where Maddie relaxes while Pammy and I get ready for work.

Every day, before I get up to shower, the above exchange takes place between Maddie and me. Literally, the same exact conversation. Maddie asks the same questions word-for-word. Only the answers change – which day, which visitor, which activity. The three demarcations of Maddie's day. And Maddie eats it up every time. She loves knowing what's coming. She's excited by the planned day ahead. And she thrives on predictable routine.

She's very much like her Daddy in that respect. I love a good routine (OK, so maybe that's an understatement). In my world, plans were not made to be broken. God does not laugh, he supports. And mice and men actually follow through as intended. Without question, I'm a sucker for a well-thought-out plan or a regular tradition. Even for the trivial stuff. If Pammy and I find a good takeout spot, what's my first reaction? "Hey, I've got a great idea, why don't we just do Chinese Wednesdays?!" Because God forbid any good thing should just come and go randomly...we must make it a part of the routine! Whether in life or in work, I always need a strategy. There's no excitement for me in the unknown.

Oh, the irony. Cue Alanis Morissette.

But no irony today. Because today was Monday. The holy grail of any good routine. And for at least one more Monday, Maddie and I each got to settle into our predictable routine. Maddie played with her Gaga and Pop Pop, took a tricycle ride to her favorite park, and smiled her way through the swing set and slides with Mommy like any other morning.

Daddy had his own version of a Monday routine today. Wake up to Maddie's sweet alarm voice. Shower. Shave. Breakfast. El ride. Phone calls. Emails. Meetings. El ride. Dinner. Dora (the Explorer), Daniel (Tiger's Neighborhood), or Doc (McStuffins). Bedtime routine. The peaceful perfection of predictability. Normalcy is my Nirvana.

The year ahead is going to bring immense challenge (yes, another understatement). But perhaps most fundamentally, Maddie and I are going to both need to learn how to live in a land utterly lacking in any sense of predictability, peace, control, or routine. Chaos will be our new world order.

While I'm not quite sure yet how we're going to navigate these choppy waters, I do know the one constant that we are tasked with providing for Maddie. Sure, there might not be the predictability of walks to the park. There might not be consistent daily activities. There might not be the clockwork evening break for Triple D (Dora, Daniel, or Doc). But through all of the chaos, there will be Love. Our unending and intense love and support for Maddie will be the rudder that guides us through the eye of this unpredictable storm. Hey, if I find an opportunity for a good tradition, I'll hang on as long and hard as possible. That's my specialty.

Turning to steadfast love in the face of so much unpredictable pain. Isn't it ironic?

The Eve of Battle (5/9/17)

G rowing up, I was obsessed with motivating myself before big challenges. Years later, it's now obvious that the word "challenge" is relative. But at the time, this meant the day before a final exam, the morning before a playoff baseball game, or the moments before my nerdiest of endeavors, a big debate matchup (I know, set your DVR now!). Oh, the crises of an average adolescence.

Nonetheless, since I was old enough to grab a remote, my source of inspiration always came from motivational movies. Before college, the *Rocky* series was my flavor of choice. Nothing pumped me up more than seeing Rocky take down Ivan Drago (and I'm pretty sure the entire Communist regime) after his intense Russian wilderness training. Or for you obscure *Rocky* fans out there, I got an even bigger rise out of the *Rocky V* street brawl, as an aging, concussed Rocky knocks out Tommy Gunn, the cocky, young, mentee-turned-backstabber. If you don't get choked up when Rocky lifts himself from the Philly back-alley asphalt at the sound of Mick's voice from beyond the grave, you have no soul.

In my college years, Rocky was replaced by William Wallace. As my roommates knew all too well, it didn't take much to coax me into reciting the entire pre-battle speech verbatim. Nothing like an epic battle or bout, especially one that involves a good underdog story and a motivational speech, to get me geared up for a big moment.

Tonight, I lay in my bed on the eve of a battle bigger than *Braveheart's* Battle of Stirling Bridge. Ivan Drago looks like a puppy compared to Maddie's Russian-sounding foe, Chemo. This isn't just one isolated battle, but a 52-week medicinal war that starts tomorrow at 7:30 a.m. at Lurie.

But like I said, I love a good underdog story. And our underdog is a hell of a lot cuter than Rocky Balboa. And certainly much more polite than William Wallace. She's even got a team of t-shirt toting supporters behind her (Thanks, Uncle Dougie and family for making the fun t-shirts! #teammaddie).

But don't let those curls and cuteness fool you. This bruiser is braced for battle. In the last few weeks, she's basically bested the equivalent of Apollo Creed, Clubber Lang, Ivan Drago, and Tommy Gunn all packed into one enemy. Despite going toe-to-toe with a tumor trying to terrorize her toddler body, Maddie now looks at us and scoffs. "Mommy, I can look up, and side to side...I'm all better now!" Despite the "necklace" limiting her actual movement, she's repeated that positive thinking mantra at least 20 plus times since emerging victorious in her first long round in the ring. Take that, tumor.

And over the last two days, ahead of her next big battle, what does she do? Forget chopping down trees or pulling a grown man on a dogsled in the mountains of Russia. That's child's play, Rock. Maddie is instead rocking out her physical and occupational therapy training by chasing down princess characters while walking on her knees. This girl is on fire!

Maddie's sense of optimism and courage knows no bounds. 29.2 pounds of pure passion and positivity. With Maddie by my side, I think the days of turning to motivational movies for inspiration are officially over.

PART TWO

Maddie Medical Update (5/11/17)

Team Maddie,

Thank you all for the supportive texts today! As an update, we're currently in the recovery room after the procedure to place Maddie's central line and Ommaya Reservoir (both of which will be used to administer her chemotherapy).

Maddie is doing great. She's eating a popsicle and watching *Wonder Pets* as we speak. At some point today, they'll move us to the oncology floor.

Thank you all again!

Minute by Minute (5/11/17)

Maddie's chemotherapy protocol is one-year long. 1 full year. 52 weeks. 365 days. 525,600 minutes. Yes, Broadway's *Rent* leaves me with no doubt as to how many minutes will be ticking by in our life's beyond Off-Broadway show.

Today was Minute One. While we have been to hell and back over the course of the last three weeks, Maddie made it *back*. She made it back to walking. She made it back to dancing. She made it back to being able to smile that glowing Maddie smile. She made it back home. She made it back to being Maddie.

But today, we turn back the clock. The 525,600 minutes that will pass during Maddie's calendar-sized cancer care have commenced. We are blessed that, as this first minute ticks by, Maddie is experiencing it at full strength. A possibility that I don't think any of us contemplated as we sat in the ICU waiting room just a few weeks ago. But here we are. One miracle down. And the march toward another just beginning.

Maddie had a great start to her day. With Grandma Sue back in town, Mommy and Daddy are chopped liver. I awoke to my favorite alarm ("Daaaaadddy...come geeeeeet meeeeee"), but no sooner do I pick up Maddie than does she look me straight in the eye and say, "Daddy, can we go downstairs, so I can play on Grandma's iPad?" How can my human powers compare to the soft glow of YouTube and Disney Junior at 5:30 a.m.? I'm just playing for second place. Happy as a clam with Grandma snuggled by her side, Maddie started her big journey with a little *Sofia the First*. Not quite *Braveheart*, but to each her own.

We arrived at Lurie Children's Hospital around 7:00 a.m. Maddie was a good sport. A few tears. A few fearful questions. But overall, she was one tough little matzo ball. In a matter of 180 minutes, at least 20 different professionals came in and out of Maddie's room. She spent a good 10 minutes watching and writhing as two tag-teaming nurses struggled through their multiple attempts to draw blood. And yet, as the anesthesiologist, Dr. Ryan, eventually carried Maddie in his arms to the operating room to place her central line and Ommaya Reservoir, she calmly snuggled into his shoulder. No tears. No complaints. She was ready.

Pammy and I made our way to the waiting room. We're now at 210 minutes. My mind was admittedly numb from signing what felt like endless consents and tuning out the canned recitations from the doctors of the various unspeakable risks that Maddie was facing with each procedure. But as we made our slow walk to wait, we passed Becca, one of the child life specialists who accompanied Maddie to the Operating Room.

"Maddie did great," she said.

"That's awesome. Did she say anything?" I asked.

"Ha, yes. When we walked in, the first thing she said was, '*WOW! This is a cool room!*'"

That's our girl.

210 minutes down. 525,390 to go.

After her popsicle induced recovery, Maddie finally made her way up to her own room. 570 minutes down. 525,030 to go. She tired quickly, but she was able to celebrate her first day successes with the Grandma Sue Diet – three chocolate chip cookies in a matter of five minutes. Her cousins (but perhaps not her nutritionist) would have been proud. Maddie then finished her day the same way she started...on Grandma's iPad. Followed by her usual routine of books and a few songs before laying down in an unfamiliar yet all-too-familiar hospital bed. 780 minutes down. 524,820 to go.

Clearly, there's going to be a limit to living in the moment. How to mentally approach this vast mass of unknown ahead is going to be a battle within the war. For the time being, Pammy and I are taking this "battle by battle" or "phase by phase." There are various milestones and defined challenges along the way. Set tasks to be completed to help mark our progress without getting caught up in the minutia of every minute while also not being burdened by the daunting volume of work left to be done and time left to pass.

Our first battle? Today they start Maddie's opening week of chemotherapy. Maddie will likely be inpatient for anywhere from 5-10 days, depending on whether they keep her here for the second week of treatment. We're going with the following title: *Phase One: Welcome Back, Lurie. Now Get Us Back Home Safely!* OK, maybe a little wordier than Operation Geronimo, but that's our focus right now. Get through this first inpatient stretch.

Either way, the clock has started. There is no turning back now. There are too many minutes remaining to count. But with an arsenal of cookies and an iPad, anything is possible.

A New Reality (5/12/17)

I can still see Pammy's face. I can still hear Pammy's voice. The moment we first learned from the Neurology Fellow that an MRI revealed a tumor in Maddie's spinal cord.

"Scott, am I dreaming right now? It's time to wake up, right?"

Pammy delivered this question not in a wishful way. Not in a denial way. Not in a sarcastic way. She asked me this question in such a panicked, fearful tone, I knew that she genuinely did not know whether she was in an actual nightmare or whether this was real life. We have obviously since come to know that both characterizations were accurate.

But there was still something surreal about the first three weeks of this experience. We were rocket-blasted through the entire cycle of grief. One week of nightmare at Lurie, followed by one week of the promise of a physical recovery at AbilityLab, followed by one week of a dream world at home before chemo. Utter Terror to Utopian Peace all in three weeks. The last week at home was so special that I think, for a brief moment, we all forgot about the big "C" word in the room.

I, for one, was just waiting for someone to pinch me. Just kidding, guys, they'd say. You passed your one parenthood test of grief and strength for one lifetime. A+. The pathology actually said that the tumor is benign. Surgery successful. Physical recovery successful. Boy, you're great parents. Congrats. Enjoy your family.

I think subconsciously this was the narrative I was playing out. In fact, I realized last night that, in all of my writings, I don't think I've ever said the words:

Maddie has Cancer.

I choke up just typing those three words. She doesn't have Cancer, right? She just has a "tumor." And Superman/Dr. Alden took out the tumor. Sure, she has a "necklace" to help stabilize her spine, but that will heal in a matter of weeks. And yes, we have to go through this whole chemo experience to make sure the tumor doesn't come back. But Cancer?

Yesterday, reality hit home. I emerged from the elevator on the 17th Floor. I only see one word on the map next to the elevator. *Cancer*. Walking down the halls, I can't help but peek into the other rooms. Child after child curled up into their beds. Bare heads. Pajama'd, weak bodies. Reality has never hurt more. I've seen these children before. On late night commercials. On marketing materials from St. Jude's. On trending Facebook posts that make me choke up and go to sleep thankful for my healthy family and amazed at the strength of others.

But I'm not walking on this floor as an outsider anymore. We're not visitors. Maddie, our sweet daughter, is a patient. With Cancer.

Yesterday was not an easy day. It was all too real. Up late into the night. Waking Maddie every two hours to check her diapers to ensure that the chemo was not interfering with her kidneys. Stirring at every beep of her monitors. Giving up on sleep and instead reading through the pages upon pages of informational materials delivered by our nurse practitioner.

This. Is. Real.

But something else is real. Maddie is not letting me give up. She's not letting me just cry my way through this experience. Because she is hanging in there. After a completely sleepless night due to the constant nurse wake-ups, Maddie had to get wheeled down for an MRI to confirm the proper placement of the Ommaya Reservoir in her head. Pammy and I stood by trying to cheer her on. It was like willing her to cross the road of a NASCAR race. The sounds were blaring. No doubt that, sleep deprived and post-op, I would've lost my mind going through this experience.

Not Maddie. I pick her up from the MRI straightjacket, and she looks right at the nurse and calmly delivers this beauty: "Little Dory says, 'Don't be such a Dory, Dory!'" A few steps later she spots a colorful toy on a desk. "Look at all the colors!" Two more steps and a *Finding Nemo* computer screen saver appears. "It's Marlin and Dory!" No sleep. Introduction to chemotherapy under way. And she's still delivering droplets of joy.

This is real. Cancer is real. But so is our sweet little Maddie. Real as ever. Keep on being such a Maddie, Maddie.

Another Day of Sun (5/14/17)

There's a window at the end of the hallway on the 17th Floor of Lurie Children's Hospital. Amid all the darkness that roams these halls, this beautifully placed window faces east and offers gorgeous glimpses of Lake Michigan. I catch a few minutes every morning to walk over while Maddie is sleeping, take a deep breath while taking in the sunrise, and pray briefly.

At least for the time being, the room next to this special spot belongs to a patient named Matthew. I've never met Matthew. His door is always closed for reasons I probably don't want to know. But his family leaves either special quotes by Matthew or favorites from family members. This one caught my eye:

Every day may not be good. But there is good in every day.

Amen, Matthew.

The eastside lake overlook is my way of ensuring that there is good to at least start off each day. And now these views, coupled with Matthew's note, will be my reminder that there is still plenty of good in each day to appreciate. No matter how dark the clouds above may be.

And thankfully, there was plenty of good in this day. Maddie is on the last two medications of her opening chemo round (these two medications continue through Monday). This first week's combination is the most intense, and it repeats every 3 weeks for the first 12 weeks. Pammy and I are referring to these initial rounds as the four Mega Treatments. Not surprisingly, the beginning of "Mega Treatment I" left Maddie pretty tired yesterday.

But this morning was a new day. Another day of sun, as Maddie's *La La Land* dance party anthem with Grandma and Grandpa would tell us. Maddie woke up her usual chatty self. She immediately asked for her "purple house" where she played with Peppa Pig and her family (and even invited Sofia to join the party). Perhaps more thrilling, Maddie took periodic breaks to watch her new favorite show. Hold on to your seat...

The live feed of the penguin exhibit at the Shedd Aquarium! Genius! She gets a kick out of giving the play-by-play to each penguin's polar playtime. "Daddy, this one's waddling! Mommy, they're hugging!" She's not quite Marv Albert, but it's hysterical nonetheless. And for Mommy and Daddy, while the last thing we wanted to hear at 5:30 a.m. was the latest penguin movement, nothing sounded sweeter than Maddie's personality returning so early in the morning.

As Marv would say, "She's On Fire!" Maddie continued her hot morning by taking a little walk to the 17th Floor Playroom. And wouldn't you know, what stood waiting for her playing pleasure? An enormous Arendelle castle big enough for Maddie to take up residence. This playroom would've made Elsa and Anna proud. Well beyond a Fixer Upper.

The day only got better as Uncle Mikey Boy arrived from New Jersey against all odds of Chicago weather and traffic. The over/under on the timing of Uncle Mikey Boy's arrival and the delivery of Firecakes doughnuts was somewhere around 45 minutes. Uncle Mikey Boy wanted to keep the oddsmakers guessing, so he managed to hold off until lunchtime. But that didn't stop him from then doubling down on doughnut volume.

And Maddie doubled down on her day of sun. Settling into a routine, Maddie crashed for a mega, three-hour nap (who says there's no such thing as catching up). Waking up refreshed, Maddie sang her way through a live YouTube singalong session with Uncle Mikey Boy and Aunts Jennifer and Jamie. Singing us everything from The Chipettes' version of *Single Ladies* to every *Little Baby Bum* song ever made (if you haven't heard of *Little Baby Bum*, then apparently you're not one of the 34 million people on YouTube who – at the mercy of their unforgiving children – have the song *Daddy Finger* irretrievably embedded into their brain). Nearly 72 hours removed from surgery and the start of chemotherapy, Maddie calmly enjoyed her normal evening routine of books and songs with me and Pammy. She's sleeping peacefully nearby as I type this sentence. And I type peacefully in awe.

Three days. Minimal sleep. Five different chemotherapy drugs. And somehow, someway, so much good to describe in this day. Matthew down the hall was definitely onto something.

Curveballs (5/15/17)

I love baseball. Not only was the game a huge part of my childhood, but I've always felt something magical about the sport. Certain aspects always seem to present like microcosms for life.

Enter the curveball. The Achilles' heel of many a talented prospect. Regardless of your baseball acumen, many of us may recall Pedro Cerrano, the Jobu-worshipping big bopper from the film *Major League*. Pedro's ability to hit home runs was astounding...so long as it was a fastball. Pedro tried everything to break his curveball curse. Voodoo. Sacrificing live chickens. You name it. Like many real baseball professionals, Pedro's ability to succeed hinged on his ability to adjust to the curveball.

Such is life. And life dropped a filthy, god-awful curveball on us today. Don't get me wrong, since April 21st – the mother of all curveballs – this hasn't exactly been batting practice. But despite this soul-crushing pitcher named Cancer we're facing, I was just starting to feel comfortable in the batter's box. We knew the opposition. We knew the game plan. Maddie's "necklace" would stabilize her spine for 6-10 weeks and ultimately leave her bones healed. Our doctor printed out a 52-week schema that laid out – week by week – the chemotherapy regimen. Sure, we were going to be facing 102 MPH fastballs day in and day out, but we knew what was coming. And we had a plan.

Then Cancer Drops The Curveball. "Oh, that plan?" Cancer asks. "That was because we assumed that Maddie's tumor cells were limited to her tumor site. As it turns out, the tumor cells are still visible in her spinal fluid. Floating around. Looking for a strikeout. So forget the plan I laid out for you. There's a new issue here. Instead of targeted radiation on her tumor site alone, at the end of our 52 weeks of chemo we may need to radiate her entire brain and spine. The potential side effects are severe. But if winning is survival, you may have no choice."

Freaking curveballs. I didn't see the pitch coming. It happened in a split second. My knees buckle. My head spins. I can barely lift the bat off my shoulder. What to do? Where to go? Needless to say, I replayed the pitch in my mind for days. Until finally deciding...

Not now.

A great hitter doesn't need to hit every curveball out of the park. Sometimes, he needs to learn to just keep his eye on the ball. Watch the pitch into the catcher's glove. And get ready for the next pitch.

And that's what I do. I don't have time to worry about something that will take place 52 weeks from now. I have a job to do. Stand in that batter's box and crush the wicked fastballs that I know are coming in Maddie's weeks ahead. I see the curveball. I watch it carefully into the glove. I dig my heels in to wait for the next pitch. Without ruminating on the scary arsenal that I know the pitcher is holding. Just taking it one pitch at a time.

Deputy Daddy (5/15/17)

A new Sheriff came to town today. Everyone's favorite deputy from *Toy Story*, Woody. Shiny Sheriff's badge and all, this favorite deputy arrived only as one courtesy of Grandma and Grandpa could – SDAS. Same Day Amazon Shipping. A grandparent's version of SOS. If Maddie so much as whispers something about a new character or a new toy, Grandma and Grandpa's internal alarms go off louder than Maddie's I.V. last night between the hours of 1:00 a.m. and 4:00 a.m. (really, air in the line *again???*). Gaga and Pop Pop are no different. Maddie's watching movies regularly, you say? Time for a portable DVD player, STAT (OK, so Gaga and Pop Pop are no different in theory, but perhaps just a little further behind the technological evolutionary scale. If you haven't met my dad, I have two words for you: flip phone).

In this Toy Story, whatever Maddie wants Maddie gets. Cookies for breakfast. iPad for lunch. Cupcakes for her pre-dinner appetizer. Dory during dinner. The chicken is officially running the hen house.

For Deputy Daddy, let's just say it's been a slow process for me to throw the rules out the window (even if it's a hospital window). In fairness, I'm guessing 99% of it is about hanging on to whatever control I have left. Before Cancer happened, our life was fairly predictable and regimented (save for the occasional sleep regression). We had our health. And we had our internal house rules. Even if we weren't super aggressive about enforcing much of anything, we at least had some semblance of tendencies (not watching television during dinner, not starting meals with dessert, etc.).

Cancer took whatever was left of the predictability and comfort in our lives (and certainly our tendencies) and ripped them to shreds in the most gut-wrenching manner possible. And here I am, still trying to salvage what is left of our previously organized world.

What have I quickly realized? I'm fighting a losing battle. Maddie's favorite Deputy will certainly be the Deputy who says Yes. But to be honest, that's a grandparent's job. They are not put on this Earth to be rule enforcers. They are put on this Earth for one reason – to provide uninhibited, unrestrained joy and happiness. And who am I to get in the way of that right now?

If Maddie were just a little older, I can even hear her thoughts on the matter. "Dad, cut me some slack. I've got Cancer for Christ's sake. Let a kid start off her day with a chocolate chip cookie and get over it! So I'm addicted to my iPad? You see this poison being dripped into my body?!"

OK, OK, Future Maddie. Deputy Daddy may have to interpret the laws a little more loosely these days. Because while reasonable people can disagree about the importance of maintaining some form of routine and structure in this otherwise warped world we've been dropped into, one thing remains certain: Maddie has the most loving, supportive grandparents imaginable. Period.

Both sets of grandparents have literally dropped every other obligation in their lives to support Maddie and to support us. I don't think there's a family in the world who could've rallied more unanimously and firmly for their granddaughter. They are truly a blessing in our lives (even if that means that sometimes they're also a pain in the previously rule-abiding, structured place where my Deputy badge used to be).

As Deputy Daddy puts his badge into a drawer (warning to all grandparents, this is just a temporary leave of absence and do not think for a minute that this unrule of law applies to Lily), Maddie is taking her first step toward freedom. Week One of the chemotherapy protocol ends tonight around 11:00 p.m. And word on the street is that we'll be able to come home, even if just for a couple of days, before starting Week Two and/or managing interim issues.

Maddie had an amazing day today. Playing in the playroom with Grandma, taking her blood pressure with Grandpa, and a little movie night with Gaga, Pop Pop, and Aunt Jennifer. And my personal favorite moment, watching Maddie sway her diaper-padded rump up and down the 17th Floor while stopping at each of the two nursing stations on multiple occasions just to say hi. Forget Sheriff, this little girl is running for Mayor of the 17th Floor!

Even from this sabbaticaled Deputy's view, Maddie has more important fish to fry than Screen Time. God willing, Deputy Daddy will have the honor and duty to re-enforce the rules yet again. 12 months minus 6 days from now. When this seemingly imaginary world hopefully returns to normalcy. When the only "C" word we have to negotiate in our home is Cookie.

We love you, Grandma, Grandpa, Gaga, and Pop Pop. And without question, you are each Maddie's favorite Deputy.

An Unexpected Break from Battle (5/16/17)

Toward the end of *For the First Time in Forever*, Elsa cries out to tell the guards to open up the Arendelle gates. For you Frozenites out there, it's definitely the emotional climax of the song (boy has life reached a new low when you're interpreting Disney songs). Maddie's week similarly crescendoed this afternoon upon our unexpected discharge to conclude Maddie's first round of chemo. In some ways, today was very much a day of opening up gates. A day of breaking free, if only for a bit.

The opening scene of this Day of Opening started promptly at 9:15 a.m., when Maddie stomped over to the 17th Floor Playroom as if to will the door to open 15 minutes prior to the scheduled start. Escorted by Mommy and Daddy, Maddie had her latest theme song playing as her entrance music (*Single Ladies* by The Chipettes). We assumed this was an exercise in futility. The playroom doesn't open until 9:30 a.m. We'll humor her and head out. We'll get there. Maddie will cry when the door won't open. We'll leave. And come back again later. Rinse and repeat. Hey, whatever Maddie wants Maddie gets, right?

But lo and behold, the Lurie Lords answered her prayers. In the form of the "Poop Man." Yes, the "Poop Man." You can't make this stuff up. That was how this man introduced himself to our nearly three-year-old daughter. Because apparently, he always carries with him a fossilized rock of dino dung from his time volunteering at The Field Museum. Poop Man's real name? Milt Levin. An 89-year-old World War II veteran, Milt has volunteered for Lurie for more than 25 years. He told me that his oldest son was sick at the age of 10. He was treated at Lurie's predecessor hospital, Children's Memorial Hospital. At the time, Milt made a commitment to himself that upon retirement he would volunteer for the hospital. 25 years into his volunteer service, all of which have been on the cancer floor, Milt remained true to his promise. And apparently the hospital stayed true to theirs, as Milt's son is now 62 years of age and residing in California.

But forget that little nugget of nostalgia. More importantly, Milt held the keys to the playroom. And 15 minutes early, on the prompt payment of Maddie's smiling face, Milt opened up shop. The gates were open.

Maddie's gate opening tricks did not end in the playroom either. Just 4 hours, and many "final" nurse exams later, the Lurie Gates themselves opened for Maddie and allowed us all to get a much-needed afternoon and evening at home. As the nurses unchained her central line from the dreaded Lurie Pole of Alarms, Maddie was free. Literally racing down the hallways in her hot pink shoes, no pants, and a puffy diaper sticking out of a backward hospital gown. And she couldn't have been happier.

It was not until I got home that I realized how weary I had really become from this first battle. Overwhelmed by medical data. Burdened by uncertainty. Exhausted from sleep deprivation. Dried out from low flow showers. Numbed from Maddie's middle-of-the-night nurse battles. Dizzied from daydreaming (or daynightmaring).

But as I lay in bed tonight, I am so thankful for the lack of beeping noises. Thankful that Maddie lay in her own bed without people waking her up, literally every two hours, to check her vitals and change her diapers (No, faithful readers,

Maddie's initial defeat of Darth Vitals has not proven to be a final battle. The Blood Pressure continues to be Maddie's overnight Achilles' heel). Thankful to see Maddie unchained from any electronic monitors and instead through our baby monitor. Thankful to have had the family, friend, and community support to enable us to continue to support Maddie. And thankful for every bit of that singing, smiling girl who somehow and someway is not burdened by any of these things. The girl who is dancing her way through Mega Treatment I.

Make no mistake, this will be a short reprieve. The battle continues Thursday morning at 9:00 a.m. sharp for the next non-Mega round of Maddie vs. Chemo (unless Fevers or Low Blood Counts, our two interim rivals, issue a challenge beforehand). But Round 1 went squarely to Maddie. And the prize of spending at least one peaceful night in our own beds couldn't be more beautiful.

PART THREE

Change is in the Air (5/19/17)

Transitions.

This was always a big word in our house.

For all of the tasks and milestones in which Maddie excelled, transitions were certainly not on this list. Whether it was transitioning child care providers, transitioning to change her diaper, or transitioning between activities (let alone transitioning from television or iPad to *any* other activity), Maddie always immersed herself fully in whatever environment or activity in which she was engaged and resisted fiercely any attempts to pull her from the moment. With transition as Maddie's Kryptonite, Pammy and I have known that she will need to develop a new super power very quickly. In the After Cancer (A.C.) World, she will be living in transition. Her new normal will be perpetual interruption. Maddie has milligrams upon milligrams of downright disgusting medicines to digest each day. She has a "central line" (a fancy catheter tunneling under her chest and into her veins) that Pammy and I will have the pleasure of flushing on a nightly basis. A once relaxing nighttime bath now begins with wrapping her exhausted body in Glad Wrap to keep water from invading the catheter. Bedtime stories are preceded with a methodical and uncomfortable changing of the pads on her "necklace." Her moments of joy are interrupted with heaves of nausea and exhaustion. Every peaceful and playful moment is fleeting. The days of full immersion for extensive periods of time are on hold. Transitions reign supreme.

And naturally, as the world rains interruption upon Maddie, what do her Mommy and Daddy decide to do? Let's get a Big Kid Bed! Brilliant idea, guys. Hey Maddie, forget that old crib that has been your quiet source of calm for the last three years. Put aside that you're just acclimating back to your home as a place of security. See ya, childhood. The mother of all transitions awaits.

But don't call Child Protective Services on us just yet. This transition of transitions to a B.K.B. was not a parental decision of choice. With the challenges ahead, Pammy and I knew that the days of us pulling Maddie out of her crib were dwindling. We're going to need easy and smooth access to her. So we did something we rarely do – we called an audible. With little discussion or analysis, we just ordered the bed. On a wing and a prayer. We took an old college try at referring to these new digs as her "Princess Bed." We dropped a Daniel Tiger pillow at the foot of the bed. And held our breath.

And wouldn't you know. She loved it! Last night, Maddie didn't want to leave her Princess Bed. She just kept calling for different family members to come upstairs and lay down next to her. And ultimately spent a pretty peaceful night sleeping in her new Princess Bed.

There couldn't be a more critical time for Maddie to be able to deal with transitions. The raindrops of change will soon begin to downpour. Body changes. Hair changes. Energy changes. Health changes.

My hope is that Operation Princess Bed is only the beginning of Maddie's newfound ability to tackle a tough transition. Because while her ability to tolerate physical transitions has been a challenge, Maddie's mental strength is unquestioned. One of the most amazing things to witness these past few weeks is how laser focused Maddie's mind is on the present. Unburdened by the fears that are paralyzing the rest of her family and friends, Maddie's life view is completely binary – she either feels cruddy (in which case she'll just lay low) or she feels good (in which case she'll be playing in full force).

Whereas the rest of us need mental "recovery time" in the face of a medical setback (either because our mind keeps us worried about the illness we just had or the illness we still have to face), Maddie's world is much simpler. Good or bad. Up or down. Tired or awake.

Take the other night for example. Maddie woke up at around 2:00 a.m. and basically vomited her brains out. If that happened to me, I'd probably have spent the next two hours talking to Pammy about how horrible the experience was or worrying about when the nausea wave would return. That pattern of worry would continue until a new, stronger experience replaced it. Not Maddie. The kid wiped off her mouth, looked up at me and Pammy, and happily said, "Mommy, Daddy, I feel better now!"

Kids. Are. Amazing. Maddie is amazing. And her mental resilience is fierce.

This morning was no different. Maddie was a little slow going when she first woke up. Waiting for one of her numerous meds to kick in, she was just experiencing some expected morning sluggishness. One hour later, as if the last couple of hours never happened, she turns to me and says, "Daddy, can we go for a walk to the park? Can Mommy come too?" So there we were, 7:30 a.m., walking Maddie down the sidewalk in her hot pink Jessie PJs (Jessie from *Toy Story*, of course) toward the park. We played for 30 minutes. And each minute was magical. The same kid who has been living with vomit by her side for the past 72 hours wanted to do nothing but get pushed "faster" and "faster" on the swing. Wouldn't that have been your first choice?!

Her swinging smiles were incredible. Pammy and I pushed her back and forth (Pammy facing her, me behind her, and us enveloping her in love). We were smiling through our tears. And watching in awe (while certainly pushing down our deepest fears and sadness) as our little princess, fresh off her first night's sleep in her Princess Bed, swung high in the air without a worry in the world. Swing high, Sweet Madeline. We could learn a thing or two from you.

Maddie Medical Update (5/19/17)

Team Maddie,

Maddie returned from the playground to go toe-to-toe with Week 2 of her chemo treatment. Unlike last week, this week's battle is only one day. Her blood counts were good, and her spirits were up. Better yet, they released her to go home this evening. Her next treatment (Week 3 of 52) is not until next Thursday. The name of the game between now and next Thursday is side effects. This is the stretch of time when her blood counts are expected to drop. When she is going to be most susceptible to fevers. It's all par for this crazy course we're on, so Pammy and I are ready either way. And we have no doubt, no matter what the week brings, there's a cute little girl just waiting for her next moment to smile.

Through Maddie's Eyes Only (5/20/17)

Emergency. Add that to the long new list of concepts that are all relative. In my day job as a divorce lawyer, even judges have a wide spectrum of concepts they find to be emergencies. Cutting someone off of a bank account? Denying parenting time? Parental misconduct? Reasonable and unreasonable judges would reach different conclusions.

One month ago, we experienced a true, unambiguous emergency. No judicial interpretation necessary. That night came with a range of emotions that I've pretty much bled on these pages.

Two weeks into Maddie's chemo treatment, emergency is now just part of our weekly routine. Any time Maddie has a fever of over 101 degrees, we go to the emergency room immediately. Any time she has a temperature of 100.5, two times or more at least an hour apart, we go to the emergency room immediately.

Normally, there's a natural fear on the way to the E.R. At a minimum, some underlying anxiety. Not tonight. At 2:30 a.m., Maddie woke up. 100.5. One hour later, per the instructions, we check again. 100.5. Pammy and I proceed to calmly finish up packing our bags (most of which are pre-packed to no surprise of our closest family and friends). I place the bags in the car gently. I walk, not run, back into the house only to tiptoe into Maddie's room to pick up

Maddie softly and place her lightly into the car seat. Pammy and I make our way down Lake Shore Drive. In the quiet enjoyment of a peaceful moment of silence with the moon glowing off the lake.

Talk about adjustment. We're both clearly settling in. And in some ways, we're just learning to see the world through Maddie's eyes. She doesn't know the meaning of an emergency. She doesn't know the significance of a drop in blood counts. She knows what she sees. She knows the tone of our voices. She knows the look on our faces.

And we now owe it to her to stay calm in the face of emergency. Because of us, Maddie just had a normal (albeit super early) drive down a recognizable street. "Look Maddie, there's Gan Shalom (Maddie's preschool)!" "OK, we're at Lurie's Place (our fictitious, fun replacement name for Lurie Children's Hospital). They called and wanted to see you today."

As I lay typing, Maddie is fast asleep on my chest in the hospital bed. Antibiotics flowing. Waiting for a room. A whole new way to experience an emergency. Through Maddie's eyes only.

Maddie Medical Update (5/20/17)

Team Maddie,

Thank you for your texts after this morning's post. As an update, Maddie was admitted into the hospital as expected. We saw a few familiar faces, and Maddie can't wait to play in the 17th Floor Playroom. And I've only walked accidentally into our room from our last stay three times so far. Sorry, neighbors!

As an FYI, this is all to be expected. Maddie's blood counts are going to drop as part of each Mega Treatment round, which will then likely cause a fever, which will then bring us to the hospital for an indeterminant number of days to prevent infection. This stay will give us a decent indication of how long it actually takes Maddie to recover absent an infection.

We'll be sure to keep you posted on her progress. Thank you all for your amazing support. For now, back to our friend, Daniel Tiger.

Chatty Maddie (5/22/17)

Maddie is a talker. And I mean a *talker*. Whether with friends, family, strangers, or Disney character figurines, Maddie loves to carry on conversations. In the age Before Cancer (B.C.), once Maddie made her way into our bed, and asked about the day ahead, Maddie would like clockwork start directing a scene from her preschool class (the same scene every time):

"Daddy, you be Zachary. Mommy, you be Georgia. And I'll be Miss Beth. OK, ecchhheeem [clears throat]. I need to have a sip from my water bottle. OK, here we go..."

At which point Maddie/Miss Beth would proceed to sing one of her favorite songs from class.

In the era of A.C., Maddie's chatty levels are also our best internal gauge of how she's feeling. Unfortunately, this weekend, the chatty levels were hovering somewhere around the level of her white blood cell counts. Maddie would wake up not to a song, but to a whimper. No role playing. Just painful squirming. She found a few minutes of comfort from Uncle Mikey Boy's smiles and the "cool games" on Uncle Dougie's phone, but unfortunately the ickiness factor stuck with her for quite a bit this weekend.

For Mommy and Daddy, having Uncle Dougie and Uncle Mikey Boy around this weekend was a much-needed boost. We were well fed (and of course well doughnuted), and Mommy got some well-deserved time to see real sunlight. I can't thank you both enough for the support and reprieve.

But also for Mommy and Daddy, who are so used to seeing Chatty Maddie 24/7, staying in the moment becomes much harder once one day of yuck starts turning into two...and then three. When Maddie is feeling and acting like Maddie, we've become pretty adept at tuning out the broader reality looming in the background. It's the pockets of Maddie's sunshine that keep us going.

That sunshine came unexpectedly with this morning's sunrise. At 5:00 a.m., I woke to a much needed request.

"Daddy, can you get my Dory characters?"

In the B.C. World, I can tell you what my response would be: "Maddie, it's still nighttime. Time to go back to sleep, and we can play in the morning."

A.C. Daddy?

"Yes! Of course, Maddie!"

This was the first time that she asked proactively to play with something other than an iPhone, iPad, or television all weekend. I knew that was no coincidence. That's our sign. And sure enough, no sooner did I break out a plastic Dory figurine from our collection than did Maddie get rolling.

"Daddy, where's Hank? And Bailey? And the otters?"

15 minutes of interactive role playing later, Chatty Maddie resurfaced. In fact, since Chatty Maddie awoke from

her slumber of silence, her fever has been down (without Tylenol) for the past 12 hours. Her white blood cell count is still low, but it began to creep up this morning. We likely have 2-3 more days inpatient as everything returns to "normal," but as we continue to get Chatty Maddie back to full verbosity, that will no doubt get easier.

I don't know what today will bring, but I do know this was the greatest gift we could've received to start our morning. Hopefully there are a few more pockets of sunshine just waiting to peek out.

F'n Ns (5/23/17)

Nurse: How's it going?
Me: You know, doing the best we can.
Nurse: Yeah, these F'n Ns are pretty rough.
Me: F'n Ns?
Nurse: Fever and Neutropenia Stays.
Me: *Oh, F and Ns!* I think I was still right the first time.

Add another nickname/abbreviation to our growing Lurie Dictionary. F&Ns. Doxo. Ceftaz. ANC. The list goes on. Pammy and I are slowly becoming experts in an area that we would've been happy to leave for others more qualified.

But yes, our first go at dealing with one of the main side effects of Maddie's chemotherapy – Fever and Neutropenia (specifically, a low absolute neutrophil count) – is probably best described as F'n Ns. Apparently, it's a pretty long haul on these F'n stays. We arrived at Lurie's Place on Saturday around 4:00 a.m. We're now at Tuesday morning with no meaningful line of sight for checkout. Yesterday's Dory Session turned out to be a false recovery alarm. Plus, the rules for dealing with F'n Ns require Maddie to be fever-free for at least 48 hours and her neutrophil count to start ticking up. Flash back to last night around 3:00 a.m. Maddie spiked a 100.5 temperature...F'n Ns!

As lengthy as the stay feels, it's at least comfortable. We're getting to know the employees at Lurie's Place really well. Other families come and go, but we exchange a few empathetic smiles. The nurses are phenomenal, and the consistent familiar faces bring calm to each day. Plus, the special visitors that grace our stays are always a special treat (thank you, Cousin Amy, for trading life in the Beltway and Bermuda for babbling about blood counts and bringing smiles to sweet Maddie).

Most importantly, despite her cruddy factor, Maddie is settling in nicely. The always touch-and-go blood pressure has become one of her new favorite challenges. Last night, after being woken abruptly from her slumber, she happily smiled and stretched her arm out for Lashonda to do her blood pressure business. It was an adorable end to the night, and I'm smiling now just revisiting. Pockets of sunshine.

Unfortunately, the only remedy for F'n Ns is the passage of time and attempting to boost her counts. And of course, since we're talking about F'n Ns, how else to boost her counts than to require *a daily injection into the fatty part of her leg*. Sure, why not! At this point, I should probably just be glad it's not a minor surgical procedure.

The icing on the cake? Who better to arm himself with such a scary syringe than...you guessed it...Deputy Daddy! That's right. Maddie's go-to way to deal with certain hospital horrors is to ask, "Can you do it, Daddy?" Or, "Can you do it, Mommy?" Daddy pulled the short straw on this particular task. When the nurse flashes the needle, Deputy Daddy to the rescue.

As I pull the syringe from its plastic pocket, the protective fatherly feelings flood my mind. Can I do it? What if I miss? Is it possible to hit muscle? Is she going to start to hate me? OK, you can do this. Deep breath. One, two, three...ALL DONE!

Splash down. A few tears. Wait to see if resentment builds. Thirty minutes later, as I wait for the PTSD to start raging on Deputy Daddy, Maddie rolls over and softly asks, "Daddy, will you come lay with me?" Deep breath again. I don't think I could love you any more, Maddie.

As Maddie and I snuggle to sleep, Maddie goes on to have one of the more restful evenings yet. It's 7:40 a.m., and she's now only just waking up with Mommy cuddling by her side. No matter how hard you may try, F'n Ns, you can't take away these gentle moments.

Fast Forwarding (5/24/17)

During one of the earlier scenes of *Finding Dory*, Marlin and Dory find themselves lost in a dark, scary part of the ocean. Without warning, a big, scary eyeball appears a few feet from their frightened, fishy faces. In just a few quick seconds, the giant squid will chase Marlin and Dory on a swim for their lives. But Maddie won't let it get to that point.

"Daddy, can you skip it?" she asks.

Faster than you can say "Dory!" Daddy grabs the remote and fast forwards through the two minutes of terror embedded in this otherwise light, funny journey. Deputy Daddy to the rescue again.

As parents, most of us have the luxury of skipping through the scary parts. We can shield our children from the ugly side of life (especially things they're too young to comprehend). We don't do this to deceive. We do this to protect. Until they're strong enough and mature enough for the complete view.

I can't even begin to describe the pain that comes with not being able to hit fast forward on Cancer for Maddie. Frankly, I'd like to fast forward for all of us. But there is no avoiding the inevitable side effects of such an intense, chemotherapy regimen. We've been blessed, thus far, to have a pretty consistent wave of ups and downs. No down was ever so long that we couldn't grit through it. While not subject to the beauty of the fast forward button, these downs felt fleeting enough that we could at least shield our eyes from the scene until that smiling Maddie returned.

The past 24 hours have felt a little different. Repeated stomach pains. Excruciating mouth sores. On and off fevers. In an effort to shield your eyes – and effectively fast forward you – from what poor Maddie is experiencing, I won't belabor it. Only so many need to share that burden. But Pammy and I can't hit pause for Maddie. We can't fast forward. The best we can do – and what we will continue to do – is just console our sweet Maddie. Letting her know that she always has someone by her side as the giant, scary eyeball of Cancer/Chemo follows her more closely than that god-awful squid.

While we can't eliminate the pain, Pammy and I know that our presence brings comfort, as we alternate responding to Maddie's quiet and repeated nighttime request: "Daddy/Mommy, will you come lay with me?" And Pammy – Maddie's absolute rock – doesn't waver for a minute through the choppy waters of Maddie's recent days. The squid might be tough, but he's got nothing on Pammy.

Fortunately, despite being in the midst of one of the scarier scenes of Maddie's journey since surgery, there are still moments of light. Moments when the sun brightens the dark bottom of the ocean. Yesterday, one of those moments came when a group of volunteer singers stopped by Maddie's room. Despite all of her discomfort, Maddie mustered the strength to enjoy a few minutes of light. Leave it to Disney cover songs to coax a smile or two.

As today's sun rises, we pray that the side effect squid goes on his merry way in the next couple of days. And that Maddie gets to enjoy a few days of swimming around with the light-hearted Dory, Nemo, Bailey, and Destiny before the squid inevitably returns.

But either way, one thing is certain. Just like Dory, Maddie is not going through this journey alone.

Maddie Medical Update (5/26/17)

Team Maddie,

As Maddie begins Day 7 of her first F'n Ns stay, we start the morning with a bit of good news. Maddie's counts are all headed in the right direction, and she was fever-free during the night.

Late morning, Maddie will receive her third week of chemo treatment (just another one-day treatment). TBD on how much longer we'll be at Lurie's Place (as next Thursday's treatment is the second of four initial Mega Treatments), but we're hopefully swimming back to the top of the ocean for at least a couple of days.

Love to you all!

Breaking Down (5/27/17)

Breakdown.

There are all too many combinations and meanings of applicable words packed into this word. Break. Down. To break. To be down. To stay down. To break away from being down. To have a breakdown. To have a break. To break something down. In some ways, the manipulation of this one word encapsulates the cycle of coping with life A.C.

As a parent, half the battle of Maddie's battle is just learning how to approach the battle. Accepting the cyclical reality ahead and breaking down experiences is critical. Never get too high. Never get too low. Every yin will have a yang. At the end of every storm is a rainbow. I could go on. But here's a less philosophical way to explain how we're able to ride the wave on our end:

You have to break it down to avoid breaking down.

Now, before you all think this word play is just a sign that I'm starting to lose my mind from the sleepless nights and constant beeping (OK, so maybe that's part of it. I am typing this on my iPhone at midnight after watching Maddie's oxygenation levels fluctuate on her monitor like I'm in charge of overseeing a top secret CIA operation), let me explain.

The emotional and durational enormity of Maddie's situation is overwhelmingly huge. If you get caught up in the mental abyss of trying to truly digest and analyze the "C" word, its impact on Maddie, its impact on all of our lives, and the road ahead, your mind will swallow you whole. It's the darkest of black holes. And the gravitational pull tries to reel in even the strongest of us, especially when things are looking grim.

It will break you. It will bring you down. It will cause breakdown.

But one of the escape hatches from that black hole has been to break down the larger journey into smaller parts. Little victories. Mini cycles. In some ways, it's no different than any major undertaking. Whether it be tackling a long-term work project or preparing for a big game, the mental approach is imperative.

Let's break this one down. In Maddie's 52-week season of chemotherapy, there are four initial, consecutive "mega" cycles. Basically, Maddie's little system gets rocked every three weeks with an unimaginable chemical intensity. Today, we remind ourselves that the first of these four cycles ended. As the sun went down on this Sabbath evening, we broke from the broader journey and came down to celebrate the success of this milestone.

Break. It. Down. Four mega cycles. One in the books. I feel like a football coach keeping his team focused on a pivotal game. Let's concentrate on winning each quarter. The game will then take care of itself. Tonight we walk off the field holding one finger high in the air. The first quarter of the first big game in this incredibly long season ahead is over.

Maddie certainly has her battle scars to show from this quarter. One week later, we're still at Lurie's Place. The opposition has hit hard. It's broken Maddie's perpetual peace. It's disrupted Maddie's restful sleep. It's robbed Maddie's childhood. It's removed Maddie's hair. It's rocked Maddie's world.

But rest assured, it hasn't taken Maddie's spirit. Maddie keeps on fighting. Bloodied not broken. She hasn't had a fever in more than 24 hours. Her blood counts are ticking back up. And on the heels of an incredibly painful week, Maddie played her way into the evening. Role playing with Peppa Pig and family. Cracking Maddie-sized smiles that I haven't seen since admission. Pausing to take bites of a cookie.

As I reflect on this all too intense week, I put down my phone and pause to watch Maddie sound asleep in her hospital bed next to Pammy. Both of them resting peacefully. Both of them beautiful. A picture would be too dark to do justice. But their soft silhouettes themselves tell the story.

In this moment, we are not down.

In this moment, we are not broken.

Blowing Bubbles (5/28/17)

In the B.C. Days, Pammy and I were pretty appreciative parents. We are not the story of that family who took something for granted only to gain appreciation after the fact of tragedy hits home. Quite the opposite. We pretty consistently stood in awe of Maddie. We celebrated each milestone and smiled at each idiosyncrasy.

And unlike most families, Pammy and I witnessed all of these moments *together*. Whether it was the morning routine, activities, or bathtime, we did everything *together*. And we experienced Maddie's first two and a half years of life *together*. It might not have always been the most efficient way to live (especially as two working parents), but it certainly was magnificent.

B.C. Maddie was one of those special kids where you didn't want to miss a moment. She was pretty much almost always happy. Always smiling, laughing, saying something cute, or being silly. In every sense of the word, she was (and is) a dream child. Sadness or irritability were reserved for three moments: diaper changes, overtiredness, and turning off the television. That was it.

One of the more difficult parts of life A.C. is watching the exception threaten to become the rule. Maddie's baseline state in this F'n Ns challenge – with good reason – is sadness, irritability, pain, anxiety, and/or fear. It's just heartbreaking to watch no matter how much we know the reason. Especially because it's so polar opposite of the Maddie we know is in there clawing, scratching, kicking, fighting, and screaming to come back out.

As a result, we're all guilty of consuming our time with her by craving that next miraculous moment. Trying to find the turning point where fear gives way to joy. Where her pained look flips into a smile. With every passing day, our craving only increases (and as a result, the lack of change only hurts more). As this lengthy hospital stay has worn on, I had begun to resign myself to the need to change my expectations. To rework nearly three years of expectations that Maddie = Happy.

Not so fast. Just as F'n Ns were in the process of erasing the Maddie Equation from our family blackboard, there she was. We had spent the entire day trying to manufacture Maddie's mental state. Trying to find Maddie in our own ways – doughnuts, jokes, smiles, toys. Nothing worked. And just as she was going to sleep, Pammy and I handed Maddie a little container of bubbles. Ironically, we gave her the bubbles not as a final, Hail Mary attempt at finding fun, but because the doctor recommended previously that we have her blow bubbles to improve her lung function (and up until bedtime, we had forgotten to try).

I have no idea what those bubbles did for Maddie's lungs. But my god did they fill up our empty hearts. Maddie smiled her way through the bubbles. They weren't smiles masking pain. They weren't smiles overcoming fear. They were just vintage Maddie smiles. Pure, unadulterated joy.

Maddie = Happy.

Who would've thought. One little bottle of bubbles at 9:00 p.m. And Pammy and me, once again sitting in awe and appreciation of Maddie, *together*.

Let the Sunshine In (5/29/17)

olidays. Three-day weekends. Weddings. Sunny, summer days with family at either Montrose Beach in Chicago or Long Beach Island in New Jersey. In the days B.C., these were the moments for which we lived. The special celebrations and breaks that removed us from our daily routines.

A.C., it's hard to find comfort in the joys of the B.C. World. Yet oddly, I have become quite comfortable in the hospital setting. A place that used to make me want to vomit upon admission. Instead, I now feel right at home the moment I walk into the building. I'm focused on Maddie. I'm on alert for medical updates. I'm locked in on conversations with the medical staff. In some ways, I'm very much in a groove here and don't spend much time stuck in my mind (outside of these writings, which take place when Maddie is sleeping).

One aspect of B.C. life that has proven especially difficult to re-embrace is my social or entertainment life (or more accurately, the previously social or entertaining aspects of my existing life). Small talk. Listening to the radio. Non-Maddie related conversation with family or friends. Cruising down Lake Shore Drive. In the past month, the moment these social or entertainment settings arrive, my mind wanders. To Maddie. To sadness. To loneliness. To simply unfocused mental space. It's so counter-intuitive because these are such wonderful opportunities to escape and re-center and yet it's precisely when I digress. Perhaps because my mind wasn't yet ready to escape. I didn't want to re-center. I had a singular focus in my free time – Maddie.

Fast forward to yesterday. One of the most special people in my life was getting married. And getting married to an absolutely amazing person at that (less his Buckeye allegiances). It was one of those weddings where you knew everyone felt the same way – that these wonderful people deserved each other – and as a result it would be a magical, loving evening. The wedding was at 5:30 p.m. And many of my closest friends would be there.

As the day grew closer, I never had a doubt that I would be going. My love for the bride and groom wouldn't allow for an alternative. I just worried whether I would have the strength to avoid turning the happiest moment of their lives into something sad on my account. Could I hold it together when embracing my friends in attendance? Could I keep the focus where it belonged that evening? Could I let friends in? Could I let conversation in? Could I let light and love in?

Just a few days prior, I would safely have said the answer would be no. That I would cry the moment I met eyes with a close friend. That my mind would wander at the first cocktail conversation.

But I was committed to a different narrative last night. Sure enough, the moment the beautiful processional began, I settled in. The ceremony was perfect. The bride and groom were illuminating in that way only a special couple can shine. And for the first time in a month, I absorbed that light. Mazel tov, Jesse and Sam. You two are role models for us all. And I was blessed to be a part of your magical evening (and selfishly thrilled that instead of bringing down the mood in any way, I was able to enjoy every minute).

Just as the light of my friends' nuptials filled my heart, Maddie jolted us with an added dose of light today. Following up her smiley evening, Maddie woke up this morning ready to roll. She played on her feet – characters in hand – for three straight hours. You read that correctly. Three straight hours. In the past week, I do not know if she did anything for three straight hours other than feel discomfort. But today, with each passing minute, you could see her shedding the side effects. Walking. Talking. Drinking. Smiling. Playing. Crafting. Eating. Napping. Socializing. And in a final symbolic move, the nurse even disconnected her central line from her other appendage – the metal tower of hanging medicinal bags. Until next time, tower of terror.

With the chemical barrage no longer bringing her down, Maddie had no problem letting the sunshine in. She played beautifully. And we all watched thankfully. Barring any setbacks, we'll spend at least one more night at Lurie's Place before capping off our lengthy stay. We're set to check in again at some point Thursday through next Tuesday for the next Mega Treatment.

While we won't be rating this stay on TripAdvisor any time soon, Pammy and I certainly grew up fast over the course of our first F'n Ns stay. Slowly building up the mental and physical stamina we'll need to continue to provide Maddie the strength and support to keep her going.

And if Maddie's current sunny smiles will be awaiting us at the end of every stormy visit, I have no doubt it will be just the reenergizing we need to keep going. And better yet, to give us a path next year to spend a sunny, summer three-day holiday weekend, as a family, enjoying the actual sunshine on the shores of Montrose Beach and Long Beach Island.

Maddie Medical Update (6/1/17)

Team Maddie,

After 12 straight days at Lurie's Place, Maddie returned home this afternoon. Even better, the powers that be decided to push this week's Mega Treatment II (previously scheduled for tomorrow) to Tuesday. That means six nights at home. We're not sure of the next time that will happen, so we're just going to try and enjoy every minute. As always, thank you all for your support. We couldn't do this without you. Until next time, Lurie's Place.

PART FOUR

This Used To Be My Playground (6/3/17)

Home again.

What a blessing. Six straight nights at home. Sleeping in our own beds. Eating from our own dishes. Showering in our own showers. For Maddie, there are no nurses waking her. There is no beeping. There are no hospital gowns. She is not restricted to one wing on one floor. She has her full cast of characters lining her playroom instead of a shortened hospital roster. She has her spot on the couch. Her snacks. Her special path to her playground. Her sister. Her family. Her home.

We are trying to, and certainly will, cherish and hold on to this homecoming for quite some time. It's a taste of what we hope is one day waiting for us again. But at the same time, Cancer has left its mark on home. Cancer has followed us inside. While home provides shelter from the storm, there is still a "what once was" feeling with being home. Because while Maddie has left the hospital, the hospital has not left her.

Cancer's infringement on Maddie's innate toddler desire for independence is relentless. Every couple of hours, a syringe of liquid medicine takes the place of her milk. Every afternoon, an uncomfortable saline flush of her central line hits Maddie on the couch previously used just for watching television. The joy of a full bath, filled with toys, splashing water, and uninhibited emotional release is limited to a little girl, wrapped in Glad Press'n Seal (to protect her central line), being hand-washed in 2 inches of water. The quiet bedtime routine of books and songs has a new pal – TPN (Total Parenteral Nutrition) – a liquid bag of nutrition that Pammy hooks up to Maddie's central line, which is then infused for 12 straight hours. Sleep means waking up at 1:00 a.m., 4:00 a.m., and 7:00 a.m. for diaper changes on account of the excess, overnight fluids.

One of Maddie's favorite phrases used to be, "What are we doing today?" Sadly, with her ever-present, palpable fear of the panoply of prophylactic measures pushed upon her, Maddie now instead asks, "Are we not going to do anything?" Translation: are you going to invade my space? Can you please just let me be?

Thankfully, while we now view home through a different lens, there is no question that this time still offers healing and strengthening for us all. To restock our physical and mental artillery before the next round hits hard. For Maddie, this means being able to be a kid again. To again dip her toes into the metaphorical toddler pool.

Every day, she's taken her favorite walk from our home to the local elementary school's playground. She happily walks along, despite her newfound weakness and frailty, pointing out her various garden friends that line the homes along the way. "Look Mommy, there's the moose!" "Oh, there is the goose!" "I found the bunny!" "Is the turtle there today?" Anyone who has joined us for the 5-minute walk (or more accurately, what would normally be a 5-minute walk that instead transforms into a 20-minute creative exploration with Maddie) – north on the street outside our house to the local elementary school playground – knows that the journey is just as fun as the destination.

To Maddie, this walk is what being home is all about. For these 20 minutes, as the sun shines down on our faces, and as the smell of summer in Chicago replaces the smell of saline flushes and sanitizer, we are all home. Tonight, Maddie was able to take that walk with her good friend, Evie. They smiled. They laughed. They played. They raced. They pretended.

What a blessing.

Home again.

I Hope… (6/4/17)

Today is National Cancer Survivors Day. If you asked me just a few months ago what takes place today, I'm pretty sure I would say it would be nothing more than June 4th. Just like any other day. But today, June 4th has become a symbol of hope. A prayer for what we desperately wish to be celebrating in June 2018 and beyond.

I'll be honest. I don't spend a lot of time thinking about the future right now. For one, my brain just doesn't have the capacity. We have so much on our mental and physical plates as is, there's just not enough space to allocate to anything beyond what we have to do in the next 15 minutes. But also because I know that starting to ruminate on the future is that dark abyss that is not worth circling. You can't expect to forecast into the future and just long for the light without feeling that crushing pain of the darkness. So I don't. I focus on the now. On getting through each day. And so far, at least for the sake of self-preservation, it has served me well.

On this National Cancer Survivors Day, however, I am sharing my most sacred prayer. Because today is not a day for my fears. But for my deepest hope. That this is just part of Maddie's story. That this is a chapter not a conclusion. As my mom's good friend – Sue Greenberg – has said, that this is just the comma in Maddie's life, not a period. That the giggles, the laughter, the playfulness that we witnessed in full effect this weekend is the prize waiting at the end of this hell. That Maddie truly is a one in a million child, and that this one in a million diagnosis will just be another awe-inspiring piece of her one in a million story.

Not only do I hope that every little thing is gonna be alright. But I hope that every little thing that has seemed to "happen for a reason" is real. I hope it's no coincidence that Maddie happened to develop a rash on her hands, which prompted us to go into the emergency room on April 20th instead of just thinking we could wait out her symptoms. I hope it's no coincidence that the neurosurgeon on call that day – our Superman (or "Super Doctor" as Maddie says), Dr. Alden – happened to be my friend's neurosurgeon. I hope it's no coincidence that Maddie's first hospital room number happened to be 1918 (the year the Red Sox and the Cubs, whose hometowns link Pammy's family to my family, played in the World Series). I hope it's no coincidence that Maddie's recovery from surgery itself was miraculous. I hope it's no coincidence that Maddie's oncologist is close friends with the doctor who – in some sense – is the initial champion of Maddie's treatment protocol. I hope it's no coincidence that Maddie was blessed with the emotional and verbal skills to help work through this nightmare. I hope it's no coincidence that when the home health nurse's phone rang last evening during her visit, her ringtone was none other than one of our favorite feel good songs during life A.C., *Three Little Birds*. I hope it's no coincidence that I woke up, on this National Cancer Survivors Day, and one of Maddie's favorite shows – Doc McStuffins – was running a special episode regarding a toddler with cancer (where they discussed everything from "chemo" to "being brave" in the same manner and tone in which we talk with Maddie).

I hope to hug my sweet girl next year. And the years after that. I hope to reach a point where she becomes so heavy that I can't hold her in my arms and sing her songs to sleep. I hope to see her form an unbreakable bond with her sister that rivals Anna and Elsa. I hope for Pammy and I to walk Maddie to her first day of kindergarten. I hope to watch her spend the rest of her youthful summers playing at the beach with her cousins. I hope to sit in awe as she gives her high school graduation speech. Her college graduation speech. And her medical school graduation speech. I hope to watch her grow into a young woman who is even half of the hero who she is right now. I hope to never see her grow too old. Because I hope that instead I have long passed. When she is in her 90s. Telling her friends how she had the best Mommy and Daddy imaginable. And that she remembers our bond, each and every single National Cancer Survivors Day, from here on out.

I hope.

Maddie Medical Update (6/5/17)

Team Maddie,

Tomorrow marks the beginning of Round 2 of Maddie's initial 4 Mega Treatments. We could not have been blessed with a more wonderful calm before the storm. Maddie truly was in a happy, healthy mood for our entire stay at home. It was pure magic. While turning the page to tomorrow is bittersweet, we are beyond thankful for this stretch. Here's to Maddie coming out swinging in Mega Treatment II!

Superheroes (6/6/17)

For all of Maddie's animation fascination, she has yet to fall head over heels for a Superhero. It's kind of funny actually. Maddie is currently waging a war greater than any we can comprehend. And who is she bringing to the battlefield? Her own personal Legion of Toon – Daniel Tiger, Peppa Pig, and Doc McStuffins. Forget leaping over tall buildings, donning black capes, or spinning a web of supernatural wonder. Give me a mild-mannered tiger who's coping with fears of a thunderstorm, a pig who spends her free time jumping in muddy puddles, and a doctor who fixes stuffed toys. GULP!

But that's our Maddie. Her super power? She's killing cancer with kindness and cuteness. And in all of her innocence, she doesn't even know it. Today was supposed to be a big battle. Round 2 of Maddie's 4 Mega Treatments. I spent more than a few hours brooding last night about the battle ahead. Hoping it wouldn't be as challenging as the last go around. Praying for the strength to keep moving forward. We packed our bags. Loaded up the car. Mentally prepped Maddie for the days ahead. Strolled a slightly skeptical Maddie into the revolving Lurie doors.

The result? Delay of game. Maddie's white blood counts were too low to have a fair fight. At least one more week of rest and relaxation to get our tiny prize fighter ready to roll. Mommy and Daddy's reaction? The usual cycle. Confusion.

Frustration.   Fear.   Disappointment.   Resignation.
Acceptance. Maddie's reaction? Let's blow this pop stand!

Yet again, Maddie's innocence remains her greatest
super power. While I spent the ride home thinking about
what's to come, what did Maddie want to do? Blast the *Alvin
and the Chipmunks* theme song at least five consecutive times
as she continues to try to memorize the lyrics.

Apparently, not every superhero wears a cape. Not every
superhero needs to fly. Instead, every once in a while, life
presents us with a real-life superhero. You just don't expect
her to be three feet tall.

But every good superhero also needs a sidekick. And in
today's modern era of Marvel filmmaking, at the very least,
previously unconnected superheroes can meet on the
battlefield for an epic war between heroes and villains.

Today, Maddie's villain of the day – Chemo – decided
not to show. In an unexpected twist of fate, however,
Maddie had a chance run-in with another real-life
superhero. Her new sidekick. This superhero doesn't wear
a cape. But he does don a uniform regularly. He doesn't
make webs. But he does make spectacular catches in his
own personal handheld web. He prefers a Louisville slugger
to a metal shield. His mask is instead an innocent,
welcoming smile. And yet in real life, he's just as big as any
big screen superhero.

His name? Anthony Rizzo. #44.

While some of my Cubby Blue Bleeding friends see
Anthony Rizzo as a superhero for his special powers on the
diamond, Maddie witnessed something even more amazing
today. A grown man, with the sports world at his fingertips,
taking time out of his day to visit the 18th floor of Lurie
Children's Hospital, where his foundation just donated $3.5
million to benefit families with children battling cancer.
Batman, meet Robin. Or shall I say, Daniel, meet Peppa.

And for those keeping score at home, you'll recall that Maddie's first inpatient room number was 1918. The year the Cubs played the Red Sox in the World Series. The coincidences don't stop there. Anthony Rizzo was drafted by the Red Sox in 2007, the year I moved to Chicago. Shortly thereafter he was diagnosed with Hodgkin's lymphoma. After six months of chemotherapy, his cancer went into remission. Anthony Rizzo moved over to the Cubs, at least in part, on account of his relationship with Jed Hoyer (former Red Sox Assistant GM) and Theo Epstein (former Red Sox GM who happens to live in our neighborhood). The Anthony Rizzo Family Foundation announced its amazing contribution to Lurie's just one month ago, which coincided almost exactly with the beginning of Maddie's chemo treatments. Last night, around 9:00 p.m., I read an e-mail from Maddie's incredible preschool director, Heidi. She recommended that I apply to a foundation she's been hearing about from other parents. Which one? The Anthony Rizzo Family Foundation. After reading more about the organization, I submitted the application late last evening. Less than 12 hours later, we find ourselves standing unexpectedly toe-to-toe with the Superhero himself in the Lurie's Place waiting room. And what t-shirt do I happen to be wearing? A Boston Red Sox shirt.

Do you believe in Miracles?

Peanut Butter Sandwiches (6/8/17)

I started working full-time in 2007. My first job was at Sidley Austin, a big law firm in Chicago. Professional yet cordial environment. Colleagues with unparalleled academic and professional credentials. Challenging cases. Numerous Fortune 500 clients. Pristine office space.

Life at a big law firm was anything but predictable. Yet I always preserved one element of predictability within my professional practice:

I packed my own lunch.

Peanut Butter sandwiches to be exact (OK, so I dabbled briefly in roasted turkey, but don't tell anyone. It was just a passing phase. I apologize again, PB). Forget that I was earning a real paycheck for the first time in my life. Forget that the firm had a beautiful cafeteria with rotating menus and a bright eating space. Forget the various restaurants within walking distance. Whether conscious or not, I carved out my little corner of consistency in my crusted sandwiches.

10 years later, and 7 years removed from my time at a large law firm, I am still packing my own lunch. And still fighting off the same wise cracks from my colleagues. Against all odds, my peanut butter has persevered. No

matter what the day throws at me, my nutty buddy is always by my side.

For these past one and a half months, my lunchtime routine was just one of many routines to go out the window. 10 years of lunchtime consistency vanished. Sucked into the garbage disposal of life that is Cancer. Since April 20th, I've been lucky to take a minute for lunch at all, let alone maintain my routine. Sneaking a snack here or there was an initial victory. Eventually branching out to a quick grab-n-go from a nearby lunch spot. But my PB routine remained in the rearview mirror.

For Maddie, her routines have also vanished more quickly than her Sesame Street pals can say "A la peanut butter sandwiches!" B.C., Maddie was like clockwork (and raising her was equally reliable). She was truly just the easiest child, almost from the moment she was born. Whether we're talking about her sleep habits (awake by 6:00 a.m., nap by 1:00 p.m., asleep by 8:00 p.m.), eating habits (cereal for breakfast, fruit for snack, rotating small menu for lunch and dinner...with ketchup) or playing habits (characters, playgrounds, zoo). What you saw was what you got with Maddie. Pammy and I (and her cast of caretakers) provided her with consistency and routine. She knew what to expect, we knew what to expect, and she brought her chatty, happy self to every moment.

That life has been flipped upside down. In the past month and a half, you can feel Maddie's underlying angst over what is coming next. It's like her brain is constantly assessing the situation. Is this when we drive back to Lurie's Place? Does Daddy give me a shot now or later? Is this the good tasting medicine or the bad tasting medicine? Just like her parents, Maddie has been forced to adjust to an entirely new routine, which includes a giant dose of unpredictability.

Slowly but surely, however, we are now adjusting to that new routine. We've been home for more than a week straight. We are all starting to know what to expect. We know what time the meds happen. We know which taste good and which taste bad. We know when we clean the central line. We know when we take our vitamins. We know that we are adjusting.

And wouldn't you know, for the first time since April 20th, I made myself a peanut butter sandwich this morning. It was spectacular. Don't get me wrong, the sandwich itself was beyond mediocre. But it didn't matter. The feeling of settling back into some semblance of normalcy was divine. My peanut butter sandwich represented something far bigger than a lousy lunch. It represented our adjustment. Our settling in.

And that representation was alive and well today in Maddie. Predictable. Normal. Fun. Maddie started her morning not craving her iPad, but playing with her Peppa characters with Grandma. Maddie affirmatively asked if her cousin, Taylor, could come over. Maddie played with Taylor with more exuberance than we've seen in a long time. And Maddie, Pammy, Lily, and I all had the pleasure of spending a fun, relaxing evening with our older cousins, Matt & Ali.

Today felt like any other B.C. day. A peanut butter sandwich kind of day. Corners of consistency within the chaos of cancer.

When We Get to Disney (6/10/17)

Jerusalem. Mecca. The Grand Canyon. We all have those places that are calling us *home*. The places where the spiritual or religious gravitational pull draws us in. For Maddie, there's no denying where her Toddler Holy Land resides.

Orlando.

(Cue the Book of Mormon song).

Or more precisely, Disney World (I guess the title of this entry kind of gave that away).

Unfortunately, the universe keeps conspiring against Maddie's biological need to visit Disney. Our first trip was scheduled for the Summer of 2016. These plans were foiled when the Zika virus happened to hit Florida in the weeks leading up to our trip while Pammy was pregnant with Lily. I remember Pammy and I looking at each other. *Zika, really? Of all times?*

After Lily's birth, we went back to the drawing board. Lily had yet to turn one month old before we rushed to book another Disney trip for early 2018. We figured by then Lily would be old enough to schlep around, and Maddie would still be young enough to appreciate the characters she so loved. We all now know how this latest booking worked out. The malignant reason for the latest cancellation makes the Zika story seem milder than *Toy Story*.

Zika. Then Cancer. Apparently, Mickey isn't in any rush to see the Kramer Family. You might think at this point we would just give up. Hell, at this point, even if we manage to book a reservation, I'd probably be too nervous to set foot on the plane.

But Maddie will not be denied. Almost without fail, every couple of days, Maddie tells us a little story about "when she gets to Disney." It's the same type of story each time just with different characters and different interactions.

This morning it was 6:30 a.m. "Daddy, when we get to Disney, I am going to tell Moana that my neck feels better." This is just one of Maddie's many Disney daydreams. She is always describing – with the same optimistic, longing tone – what she is going to tell either Mickey, Daisy, Goofy, Doc, Moana, Nemo, Crush, or Dory...when she gets to Disney. The excitement and enthusiasm are there each time. What's particularly amazing is that I don't know if she has any idea what a trip to Disney World actually entails. But it's calling her. Like Terence Mann walking slowly to the edges of the cornfields in Ray Kinsella's Iowa outfield. She doesn't know what's out there, but she knows she's meant to go.

For me and Pammy, "when we get to Disney" is a metaphor for all of our hopes and dreams. When we get to Disney means we have made it out of the darkness and into the light. In some ways, these reprieve weeks at home place us front and center with the life we now live versus the life we used to live or could be living.

Don't get me wrong. The joy of watching Maddie being Maddie these last couple of weeks is unparalleled. But with each adorable smile still comes a dimple of pain. Watching this little girl, getting dealt one of the harshest hands that life has to offer, still smiling. Still dancing. Still lighting up the world. It's a thing of beauty. And yet simultaneously, a soul-crushing reminder of how tragic it is that – of all people – this near three-year-old dream child has to get dragged into such a nightmare.

But we can't dwell in the sadness. Because we can't change this chapter of Maddie's life. Our only choice is to stay strong. To keep giving her the strength and optimism to have these days of unrelenting joy. To do our best to let these happier days fill our souls.

And to hope that one day we are looking back on this year as a thing of the past. As the life we used to live. As the most miraculous victory imaginable. Smiling about our story. Cherishing both our sweet girls.

When we get to Disney.

One More Song, Daddy (6/10/17)

Tender is the night.

There is no moment more tender than the 10 minutes before Maddie goes down to sleep. Maddie brings so much energy to her healthy days – the smiling, the dancing, the singing, the giggles. Maddie exudes exuberance. And to see that exuberance quietly calm before bed is soul warming (especially these days when it's not diluted by pain or nausea).

I have always treasured these magical minutes. But the amount of gold in that treasure has multiplied in the past couple of months. Every night since Maddie was old enough to rest on my shoulder, I have ended our days singing her to sleep. There are four parts to this nightly concert. First, I make my way into her room, holding Maddie tightly, while singing the *Shema*, the oldest of Jewish prayers. We then snuggle together into her rocking chair and continue with two or three more songs. The Daddy Playlist may run deep, but the rocking chair songs are recycled nightly for consistency. It's always some combination of any of the following: *The Dock of the Bay*; *Sweet Baby James*; *Tupelo Honey*; *Our House*; *Up on the Roof*; *You've Got a Friend*; *Your Song*; or *House at Pooh Corner*. Selfishly, two or three songs turn into four, five, or six if I just haven't quite had enough yet (which always seems to be the case lately). Next, I sing another song that remains constant at the middle section of the show (a customized version of an obscure tune, *And We Bid You Goodnight*), as I walk slowly from the rocking chair to the crib (now Princess Bed) bouncing gently to the beat of the song. And then I lay Maddie down comfortably. (Have I mentioned that I love a good routine?)

Without fail, even if Maddie is half-asleep, the moment her tush touches the mattress she whispers softly, "Can you do one more song, Daddy?" It's not really a question at this point. This is the equivalent of the band walking off the stage even though everyone knows they're coming back out for one final encore. We've been singing "one more song" for more than a year now. That song represents each of our last efforts to hold on to the day. To hold on to another moment with one another. And God am I holding on right now.

While the songs haven't changed over the past year, the meaning of the lyrics certainly have. Perhaps no more than the final encore song.

You know the song. It's about sunshine. On cloudy days. And a certain little girl. And a certain little month.

Truer words were never spoken. Or sung. We are in the midst of one hell of a cloudy day. It's not just cold outside. Cancer has attempted to ice over every aspect of our life. But you better believe we've got sunshine. She was born in the month of June. And Maddie's presence represents all the riches that one Daddy can claim.

As I sing this Temptations classic to end the evening, Maddie may just be hearing the same song we've been singing for months. Her final signal for bedtime. But I now hear something different. I now hear a nightly prayer. A prayer of gratitude for Maddie. And a prayer of hope for many more nights of "one more song."

In some ways, these past couple of weeks have been our family's version of "one more song." We know the cloudy days are coming again soon. Yet every day, all we are seeing is sunshine. Today, Maddie spent an unbelievably sunny day with her Aunt Risa. She had dance party after dance party. She toured Aunt Risa around her neighborhood. And she added a new character to her ever-growing figurine family, Bonnie from *Toy Story 3*. Yes, Bonnie. Not exactly flying off the shelves any more. Which is why Bonnie arrived from the U.K. via a bid by Uncle Mikey Boy and Aunt Risa on eBay. But I digress.

Maddie's dance party cup runneth over with Aunts Jamie and Jennifer joining the show, and a special guest visit from Maddie's friend, Georgia. Maddie is bringing her sunshine to these cloudy days.

We know the next Mega Treatment is soon. Absent another unexpected and unwelcome setback, it'll start up again on Tuesday. But we just want one more dance. One more smile. One more giggle. One more silly face. Before Chemo crashes the party.

We can't stop the march of time. We can only enjoy these precious moments of sunshine we are given. And continue to pray for one more song. And for that song to keep playing for years to come.

Pixie Dust (6/12/17)

Back to reality.

Or surreality.

I'm not even sure if there's a difference anymore.

Perhaps it's the mass of Disney characters living rent-free in our home. But the lines between real and surreal are narrowing. The vacillation between "how can this really be happening" and "the intense pain of this happening is all too real" is an ongoing mental struggle.

Today marks the end of an enjoyably real and particularly amazing and unexpected two weeks at home. As a family. For all of the crazy new aspects of our A.C. life, this was just a wonderful "normal" feeling week at home. Time with friends. Time with family. Time at the park. Time playing. Time napping. Time reading. Time singing. Time dancing. Time living.

For the first time A.C., Pammy and I even had moments to do the little things. The laundry list of household items previously relegated to the DBT list, a cancer-jumbled version of TBD, Delayed By Tumor. Perhaps most exciting, we took the time to reorganize and beautify both Maddie and Lily's bedrooms. More on that later. But needless to say, it felt so good to just be.

Unfortunately, the reality of getting to "just be" is coming to an end for this chapter. Back to the surreal reality of Lurie's Place. It's definitely a mixed bag of emotions. Reality tells us that it's time to get going. Reality reminds us that Maddie's next round of treatments – the same treatments that are saving her life – are waiting. Reality says that we at least know what to expect, good and bad. Reality feels like we're adjusting. Reality demands that we can do this.

But that doesn't stop the other thoughts from creeping in. When I hopped on the train this morning to head into work, my mind started to leave the station. My thoughts started bleeding on the tracks. The desire to just wish this all away. The hope for Maddie to just magically be better the moment I step off the train. The prayer that there is light at the end of the tunnel. The fear of what if there is not.

Before my mental and emotional train derailed completely, however, I pause. And remind myself. There is only one verifiable reality right *now*. And that is this:

We *are* doing this. Maddie *is* here.

That's what matters. No room to get stuck in self-pity. No room to worry about what the future may hold. Focus on our existing reality. In the present moment. Where Maddie remains a real and surreal force to keep us all going.

And thankfully, even in this harshly real experience, there's still always room for the otherworldly. Something not necessarily cloaked in tangible reality. Room for Disney dreams. Room for Superheroes. Room for Faith.

Re-enter our delayed bedroom beautification project. One piece of that project was an old wall decal. We bought the decal for Maddie's then "new room" when we moved homes in 2016. A cheesy, parental effort to get her excited about her new yet unknown bedroom.

Sadly, I can't blame cancer for the 12 months where the decal sat collecting dust in our back hallway. That was just good old-fashioned procrastination. And well justified at that (Pammy, I swear on all things pure in this world, that I will never put up another wall decal again). But this wall decal was well worth the wait.

The decal? A big pink Tinkerbell, pointing her wand downward toward Maddie's bed. She's accompanied with the following quote from *Peter Pan*:

All you need is Faith, Trust, and a Little Pixie Dust.

Leave it to Disney to remind us that the lines between the real and the surreal are not always clear. That even in this inescapable reality, there are other forces to help us through. Faith. Trust. Pixie Dust. We'll be bringing all three to Lurie's Place tomorrow. And hoping that Tinkerbell has Maddie's body and blood counts rested and ready for the next round.

Maddie Medical Update (6/13/17)

Team Maddie,

Thank you for your prayers and positive thoughts! Mega Treatment II is off to a good start. Amazingly, Maddie was in good spirits all day. At some point soon, the nausea and malaise will kick in, but for now she's just enjoying the fun parts of Lurie's Place – the playroom, the snacks, walks around the floor, etc. The interrupted sleep is always a pleasure (hence the reason I am writing at 1:30 a.m.), but she's handling it pretty well. After the nurse's latest pop in:

"Daddy, can you talk to her outside?" asks Maddie with her eyes closed.

"She already left, kiddo," I say as the nurse quietly closes the door behind her.

"Yesssssss!!!!!"

The little victories, Maddie. I love you!

Not Our First Rodeo (6/14/17)

What a difference a few weeks make. Coming to you live from Room 1705. Day 2 of Maddie's Mega Treatment II is officially in the books. Rumor has it she'll be home by Friday. It's early in the game, but Maddie has come out swinging. Mega Treatment II has an entirely different feel from Mega Treatment I. Maddie knows the ropes. She can find her way to her current room, her old room, and her room before that. She walks past the nurses' station and asks, "Where's Tim?" when she notices one of her favorite nurses isn't in his usual chair. When Justin (The Fastest Blood Pressure Pumper in the Midwest) arrives, Maddie just plays along. Blood pressure schmlood pressure, she scoffs.

The Main Event came tonight at 9:12 p.m. Maddie had a giant band-aid glued to her lower back (where they recently injected chemotherapy into her spinal fluid). It's like the nurses wanted to play a sick joke on us for all of the questions we've asked over the past month. This Tape Monster was oppressive.

Plan A was to take it off during the daytime. The next thing we know, the clock hits 9:00 p.m. My NFN (New Favorite Nurse), Christie, asks, "You guys didn't happen to take that band-aid off her back yet did you?"

CRIPES!

So much for Plan A. At this point, Maddie has been fast asleep for an hour and a half. A few weeks ago, so much as breathing on Maddie while she slept at night would cause her to jolt up in fear. Cue the tears. Cue the question. "Are you not going to do anything?"

Enter NFN Christie. "What's the game plan?" I ask.

<u>Backup Plan A:</u> Slowly wake Maddie, let her know we're going to take off the band-aid, but that it won't hurt. And hopefully build trust that she can close her eyes without worrying that even in her deepest slumber she'll be startled by pain.

<u>Backup Plan B:</u> NFN Christie slowly rolls Maddie to her side. And rips off the Tape Monster as fast as humanly possible just praying it's gone before Maddie can say, "Are you not..."

We Pow Wow. We Pause. We go Backup Plan B. Christie rolls her over. I'm watching Maddie like a hawk in case she wakes. "Crap!" I hear Christie say. "I can't get the edge lifted." Maddie starts to stir. We're running out of time. *Rrrrrrippppp!* NFN Christie pulls the Tape Monster away. Lifts it in the air in victory. Quietly skirts out the door. Just as the door is closing, Maddie's eyes gently open in confusion.

I whisper calmly, "Don't worry, kiddo, you just had something stuck on your back. Christie helped get it off."

"OK, Dadd..." Maddie slurs as she drifts back asleep.

Now that's Mega Treatment II!

Overall, Maddie is decently comfortable here this time around. What's not to like? TVs available 24 hours per day. Room service. Lake views. Playroom side housing. "Lurie's Place: Come for the chemo, stay for the memories." OK, maybe not. But it's been quite a different start than last round. I still remember watching the chemo get dripped into her central line on our first visit. I couldn't look away. Every drip felt like someone was stabbing my heart. I wouldn't let a nurse so much as step into the room without giving him/her the full tutorial on dealing with Maddie and having a full Q&A session on what they'd be doing that visit.

This time is different. The chemo is just background noise. The nurses don't look like they want to kill me. I think they may have even stopped drawing straws for who has to deal with Maddie's parents overnight. Maddie played like a champ with Mommy and Grandma all day. Come bedtime, Maddie fell asleep on me, mid-book, comfortable and exhausted in a way that never even happened B.C. As I type, I can hear (and even enjoy) the summer night Navy Pier fireworks show.

Don't get me wrong. It's not all smiles and sunshine at Lurie's Place. We know the party ends soon. The early smiles will be erased by the dreaded F'n Ns side effects. The sleep deprivation will catch up to us all. But for now, I take solace in the fact that we are getting better at this. That Maddie is getting better at this. And that the Tape Monster won't be returning for quite some time.

Maddie Medical Update (6/16/18)

What a rock star! After her best hospital stay yet, Maddie is now back at home sleeping in her own bed. Minnie covers and all. Like any true rock star, Maddie finished off her big moment with a little personal concert during her "music therapy" session. We can't get over how strong Maddie was during this Mega Treatment II. She remained largely her fun, happy self for the duration. Taking her own temperature, high fiving night nurses, and socializing with the other patients, Maddie was a breath of fresh Lurie air.

While the next two weeks will bring their share of challenging moments, we go to sleep tonight thankful for a positive hospital stay and the ability to all sleep in our own beds for the first time in four days. Rock on, Maddie!

Father's Day (6/17/17)

I am the luckiest father in the world.

You read that correctly. The luckiest in the world.

As you can imagine, this will not be a Father's Day that I will be forgetting any time soon. But standing in my shoes, in this very moment, I mean this genuinely when I say that this is a *Happy* Father's Day. For those looking in from the outside, please don't feel an ounce of sadness when wishing me a Happy Father's Day. Today is not a day for pity. Not a day to feel badly for what our family is going through. Not a day for wondering what Father's Day will feel like this year. Because I'll tell you what it feels like. At this very moment.

I feel Happy.

Genuinely. Not in a cheesy reflective way either. Happy in a "I am fortunate to be called Daddy by the single most miraculous toddler around" kind of way. Happy because, nearly two months ago, I sat in a waiting room for 6 straight hours while she underwent emergency surgery and not knowing if I would ever get a chance to see that beautiful smile again. Or hear that cute voice. Or see that silly shimmy. Happy because I watched a little girl go from near-paralysis to dancing her way through disease. Happy because I type this as my little three-year-old hero sleeps on my chest. Happy because when I come back to our real home (you know, that place where we get to sleep peacefully every so often), there's a sweet little 4-month-old, smiling and cooing her way through the bliss that is the ignorance of her infancy. Happy because I have the most amazing, strongest damn wife this world has ever seen. Happy to be surrounded by two other strong fathers in their own right. One a champion of curing cancer and the other of killing cancer with comedy.

I have never felt more acutely the joy of what it means to be a father. And the magnitude of my responsibility to provide shelter from the storm. The other night, after the nurses performed their usual nightly vitals checks, Maddie peeks up at me for reassurance. In the quiet, eerie calm of our hospital room, she asks:

"Daddy, and then all done?"

"And then all done, kiddo."

"Daddy, will you come lay with me?"

"Of course, sweet girl."

Laying together. In a hospital bed. Shielding her from any fears of what may wait outside the door. That's Fatherhood.

So yes, today is a Happy Father's Day. My life A.C. is the essence of what it means to be a father. I didn't choose this experience. But I have chosen what role I am going to play in it. And never more in my life could I be prouder to be called Daddy.

The Nook (6/20/17)

"(Insert Name), have *you* seen Maddie?"

Anyone who has spent at least 12 consecutive hours with Maddie has been asked this vexing question. Maddie, the ultimate hide-and-seeker, usually asks this question as she stands 6 inches from you with her head poking through a blanket. Let's just say she's not quite ready to be a private investigator.

What began as a cute infant trick of covering her eyes with her burp cloth developed over time into burying herself deep in blankets or constructing elaborate forts. Whatever her hiding spot, she just loves burrowing into small spaces. She finds comfort in tight, cozy surroundings.

This anti-claustrophobia is on full display when Maddie gets tired. Since she was a newborn, there was always one spot that Maddie couldn't resist. It's called "The Nook." No matter how strong her desire was to fight nap time, The Nook was always calling. It was as if The Nook had its own centrifugal force pulling her in for a hypnotic landing.

Where is The Nook you ask? On my right shoulder. Never the left. With Maddie laying her head facing outward. Never inward. As she snuggles her cheek into the space between my neck and shoulder.

The Nook is a magical place. The Nook has gotten us through turbulent plane rides, long waits at doctor's offices, and most importantly, restless nights.

The Nook is equally therapeutic for me. To feel those little hands tapping my back before she passes out. To know that this one minuscule space can bring Maddie maximum ease. To make pain go away with a simple cheek to shoulder landing. In a matter of minutes, The Nook becomes the missing Tetris piece to Maddie's unrest. The Nook is our bond. The Nook is peace.

Hence one of the many little challenges that plagued Maddie's last couple months. At no other time in her life has she needed comfort more. At no other time would The Nook have come in more handy. But for 10-plus weeks, Maddie's neck has been swallowed by her plastic collar. Put aside the stranglehold the collar put on Maddie's mobility. It was also the only thing standing between Maddie and The Nook. When I'd pick up Maddie and hold her at bedtime, I could feel her trying to manage the awkwardness of being utterly exhausted but unable to truly settle into The Nook.

But we knew there was a light at the end of this currently Nookless Tunnel. A few weeks ago, we received the go-ahead to start weaning Maddie off the collar. One hour a day for three consecutive days. Two hours a day for three consecutive days. Four hours a day for three consecutive days. This slow march to freedom continued for another three weeks or so.

The final lap came last night. Our Super Doctor, Dr. Alden, let Pammy know that Maddie was free to fly again. All day. And for the first time in two months, Maddie was also able to land. Safely. And snuggle into The Nook.

Bedtime last night was beautiful. The icing on the miracle cake that was Maddie's recovery from surgery. As Maddie burrowed into The Nook without plastic interference, I put on an epic evening concert. Five songs.

Gently lay into bed. Two encore songs. And as Maddie drifted to sleep, she whispered:

"Daddy, I'm so proud that I can sleep without my necklace."

"Me too, kiddo."

But don't let Maddie's newfound freedom fool you. After spending this morning playing (yes, playing going into Day Four post Mega Treatment II), she was back to her hiding self. Mommy and Gaga worked together to build a vintage Maddie fort. I put on my shoes and get ready to head out to work. And as I open the door to leave, what do I hear?

"Daddy, have *you* seen Maddie?"

I see you, sweet girl. Bright and beautiful. Your miracle on full collarless display.

Maddie Medical Update (6/20/17)

Team Maddie,

Maddie had a quick visit to Lurie's Place today for her Week 5 outpatient chemo treatment. Key word: outpatient! By this stage in the post Mega Treatment game in Round One, Maddie was already back in the hospital. We were in the midst of our 12-day F'n Ns stay.

In an unexpected surprise, Maddie's blood counts were high enough today and did not necessitate transfusions or hospitalization. The side effects will only hold off for so long, but in the meantime, it was another great day for Maddie.

Maddie Medical Update (6/22/17)

Team Maddie,

Well, Mega Treatment II finally kicked in. Maddie spiked her first fever this afternoon. So today marks Day One of our second F'n Ns stay. All par for the course. Good news – Maddie is in great spirits. She is just relaxing and watching *Mickey Mouse Clubhouse*. Please pray for a speedy stay!

Disney Magic (6/24/17)

D isney always gets the best of me when I least expect it. This morning, at 6:00 a.m., it was *Moana*. Maddie and I snuggled up together in her hospital bed, fired up my laptop, and watched the movie together for the first time. Well, Maddie watched. I basically cried my way through.

That's to be expected at this point. There's no doubt I'm searching for meaning these days anywhere I can find it. And *Moana* delivered as forcefully as a crashing ocean wave. For those who haven't seen the movie, the backdrop takes place in a once awe-inspiring tropical island. A symbol of all things precious in the world. Bright. Bold. Beautiful. Yet the evil powers that be begin to batter this once perfect body of land.

The viewer sees the brightness turn to darkness. The viewer sees the multi-colored flowers replaced with char.

That's what the viewer sees. I see cancer. And chemo. Trying to strip away the most perfect thing I know in this world.

But then enter Moana. Fitting her name starts with an M. The universe has called her to restore all things beautiful. To go on an unparalleled journey, against all odds. To sail into the deepest, darkest, scariest parts of the ocean. And return to deliver the beauty that once was.

Damn you, Disney. All I wanted was a mindless, restful Disney morning. Instead, I got a heart full of Disney magic. Tears and all. But my goodness was it powerful.

In my constant search for hope and meaning, I just pray that the universe picked another brave girl to lead the way. To dive into the darkest depths of the ocean that our non-animated world has to offer. To allow the chemo to burn down her cancerous cells and restore her to the bright, beautiful girl we all know and love.

When the ending credits roll, I can hear Maddie snoring as she rests on my slowly growing Maui-like belly. I guess she didn't go through the same symbolic mental exercise as me during the movie. But then I turn to the window. With the lyrics of *How Far I'll Go* still ringing in my ears, I see the view we've never had from our hospital room before. The seemingly endless line where the Chicago sky meets Lake Michigan. And now I know, more than ever, there's just no telling how far Maddie will go.

Disney Magic.

Mega Treatment II: The Birthday Miracle (6/27/17)

The sequel. Never an easy task to follow up the original story. Maddie's F'n Ns stay from Mega Treatment I was very much like the original *Rocky*. There was no winning that battle. The victory was in the journey. For Rocky, that meant "going the distance" against Apollo Creed. While he lost the fight itself to a judge's decision, he won the larger moral victory of finishing the fight against all odds. He persevered.

Maddie's story for Mega Treatment I was no different. Chemo beat her up pretty good. But Maddie's progress wasn't marked by her pain. Or fevers. Or mouth sores. Maddie's victory was in the journey. She won just by making it through all 12 consecutive hospital stay days. She persevered. She went the distance.

Like Rocky (who actually emerged victorious against Apollo in *Rocky II*), Maddie had a different tale to spin for Mega Treatment II. In the early goings, the ending was unclear. Chemo threw a wicked upper punch to start. Instead of fighting on her home turf, Maddie was forced to put up her dukes on the 21st floor (an overflow floor) due to patient overcrowding. She had unfamiliar nurses at her bedside. There was no playroom to find reprieve between rounds. Momentum was shifting Chemo's way.

Maddie was definitely hit hard. As of Monday morning, despite being moved back to the 17th Floor, she still hadn't spoken more than a few words. The pain of speech was too great. She hadn't left her bed to walk since admission. Her heart rate rose as did her discomfort. This had a lot of the makings of Mega Treatment I.

But a good sequel never turns out the same exact way as the original story. And there's nothing like a good ole fashioned miracle to change up the storyline. In our case, Pammy arrived at 7:00 a.m. on Maddie's birthday morning. Initially, this was a mixed bag of emotions. Trying to put on a happy face for Maddie's birthday. But disappointed that in lieu of a proper party, we'd be celebrating in a hospital room with Maddie incapable of so much as cracking a smile. You can only imagine the twisted emotions of celebrating your three-year-old's birthday on a cancer floor instead of a dance or gymnastics floor.

We didn't dwell in that place. We just tried to make the most of it. "The Sisters" (Aunts Amy, Jennifer, and Jamie) bedazzle the room with decorations. Amazon's "Alexa" plays tunes for inspiration (thank you, Uncle Mikey Boy and Aunt Risa). In lieu of *Eye of the Tiger*, Maddie goes with Daniel Tiger. The Birthday Fairy (cheers to Pammy for finding this amazing organization) sets up a Doc McStuffins themed party. Maddie's preschool music teacher puts on a birthday bedside concert. The hospital staff brings *Frozen* gifts. All of the optimism you can pack into one small hospital room is there beaming with birthday light.

Cue the real *Rocky* theme song...errr, Daniel Tiger theme song.

Just like that, this collective burst of fun inspired Maddie. Her turnaround was quicker than Apollo's footwork. Maddie first asks to go to the playroom. The next thing you know she's chatting it up with all of the nurses. She's showing off her new characters. Then she's standing and playing in the playroom. And suddenly she's riding a tricycle down the halls at full speed. Pammy and I can't believe this is the same kid. Just hours before, we were basically waving the white flag to another 10-plus day F'n N stay. And now we're ready to have a birthday parade down the hallways. How is this possible? How can this be? I'll tell you how...

She's Miracle Maddie. That's how.

Today's final miracle? Getting discharged. Yes, discharged. To home. On her birthday. No offense to Rocky and Apollo, but this was the best sequel I've ever seen. Happy Birthday, sweet Maddie girl. May your birthday miracles continue to carry all of us through the years. We love you.

Maddie Medical Update (6/28/17)

Team Maddie,

Just another day in the neighborhood here. Maddie spiked a fever tonight. The remnants of Mega Treatment II were still lingering. Unfortunately, protocol says we go back to the ER. We've been here since 8:00 p.m. or so. But on the bright side, this is the closest thing to a date night out Pammy and I have had in two months. Maddie is fast asleep and we're awake and socializing with the nurses. Break out the potassium chloride, party animals!

Not surprisingly, Maddie has been a rock star. She took her own temperature. She is all about the blood pressure. And she got to stay up late watching *Lion Guard*.

A quick funny story from earlier tonight. While Pammy is updating the nurses outside the room at 10:00 p.m., I'm on Maddie's third nighttime book hoping she'll fall asleep. She's overtired. In the ER. Just finished up a few sets of vitals. We're on page 53 of a 65-page book. Read that again – page 53 of a 65-page book. And I read out loud, "And he hid behind the stage..." A totally innocuous line in the book.

No sooner do I turn that page than does Maddie whisper with her eyes half open, "the sign..."

"What Maddie?"

"The SIGN!"

I turn back the page trying to figure out what in the world she's talking about. Apparently, I read one word wrong. One word. On page 53. At 10:00 p.m. From her hospital bed.

"And he hid behind *the sign*."

As always, Maddie is right. And Daddy is wrong. I'm used to that at this point. We have a late night ahead, but it sounds like after a quick transfusion and some meds we're good to go home tonight (aka tomorrow morning). For now, back to our romantic date night...

Independence Days (7/2/17)

"Is it Zoo Time?!?!"

Another classic Maddie question.

During her second year of life, Zoo Time was pretty much all the time. I still remember when Pammy and I first signed up for a membership at the Lincoln Park Zoo. We spent a bit of time deciding whether it was worth it. If I remember correctly, the threshold for which the membership benefit (free parking) exceeded the cost of just paying undiscounted parking was somewhere around 10 trips to the zoo. We debated whether that was realistic or worthwhile. Well, about 40+ trips later, I'd say the membership was well worth it. Weather permitting, Maddie spent an average of 2-3 days per week at the zoo. And it never got old.

Watching her grow along with the animals has just been awesome. Slowly the animals were bestowed names. "There's Nala!" "Look Daddy, it's Simba!" "Where's Alexander Camelton?" She knew the lay of the land. Turn right for the African exhibit. Turn left for the gorillas. You name the species, she could get you there.

For the past three months, however, no time has been Zoo Time. Or any other free time for that matter. In fact, Pammy and I realized that we haven't been on a car trip with

Maddie to go anywhere except a doctor's office or a hospital in three months. That's not an exaggeration. Three months. Our family used to go to at least three places *per day* – activity, zoo, aquarium, restaurant, park, you name it. If there was daylight, we were exploring.

Yet since April, every aspect of our lives – and especially Maddie's life – has been restrained. Restrictions have supplanted explorations. Nothing has been hit harder than Maddie's independence. Cancer has thrown every impediment Maddie's way. A tumor trying to debilitate her walking. A collar around her neck for 10 or so weeks. A laundry list of medications that has turned her home, at times, into a pharmaceutical prison. Lengthy hospital stays connected to all things beeping. Late night wakeups for vitals and diaper changes. And perhaps what is most challenging at this moment, a rigorous chemo treatment protocol that limits Maddie to 7-10 good-feeling days per month.

We are now in the midst of that 7-10 day stretch. The light at the end of each dark monthly tunnel. Because when those 7-10 days arrive, everything else fades away. You forget the pain. The vomiting. The lethargy. The crying. The sadness. They all become the past. And they're replaced by the glory that is these 7-10 days. Maddie's Independence Days.

What better way to spend those Independence Days than rekindling an old flame. Three months later, with Maddie's cousins (Josh, Seth, and Danny) in town, we were finally able to yet again make this time Zoo Time.

Hello Nala, old friend. Great to see you, penguins.

It was like jumping into a time warp. A world that we used to know but haven't been able to so much as sniff in months. And sniff today we did. Rhino poop never smelled so good! To no one's surprise, Maddie took in the whole experience. Because that's what she does during her Independence Days. She is full of every single ounce of energy that her body can muster. She dances, smiles, and sings her way through her Independence Days.

As you watch the fireworks this weekend, please keep our little firework in your thoughts and prayers. Maddie is in the midst of brightening our previously dark skies. And she doesn't appear to be slowing down any time soon. Unless it's to say hi to the penguins, of course. See you next time, Zoo Time!

Shirley, You Can't Be Serious (7/7/17)

Two and a half months ago, Maddie arrived at her rehab center, Shirley Ryan AbilityLab, by ambulance. The world as we knew it was flipped upside down. Unexpected ER visit. Followed by incomprehensible MRI. Followed by devastating diagnosis. You know the rest.

When Maddie first arrived at Shirley Ryan, she wasn't yet able to stand on her own. She had minimal use of her left hand. Still reeling from the trauma of her emergency surgery, she couldn't sleep through the night. She was hot and cold with the nurses. And she was slow to warm to the therapists themselves.

To all of our collective surprise, Maddie miraculously thrived in her limited eight-night inpatient stay. This is one of the main miracles in Maddie's journey that we reflect on regularly. One of the miracles that motivates us in moments of morbidity. One of the miracles that reminds us that the impossible can become possible.

At the time, and as I relayed in an earlier writing, our intake interviewer asked us our goals for our inpatient stay. Despite being interviewed separately, Pammy and I had one, united answer: regardless of physical progress, we wanted to preserve Maddie's spirit. Her happiness. Her love for life.

So how are we doing so far? This week, Maddie returned to Shirley Ryan AbilityLab for the first time since her miraculous discharge. Watching Maddie smile her way through her two sessions, we're reminded not just how far she's come physically. But more importantly, that we've done one heck of a job preserving our ultimate goal – keeping Maddie as Maddie.

At this moment, I am filled with pride for Maddie. For Pammy. For our parents. Siblings. Friends. Teachers. Classmates. Colleagues. And every one of you that has played a part in bringing joy to Maddie's life during this otherwise daunting time.

Make no mistake, Maddie's performance at Shirley Ryan is no accident. It's because Pammy and I are doing the job that we set out to do. And Maddie, in all of her miraculous glory, is doing what she does best.

Being Maddie.

PART FIVE

Maddie Medical Update (7/12/17)

Team Maddie,

Maddie returned to Lurie's Place today for the beginning of Mega Treatment III. At this point, if you were to follow Maddie around, you would genuinely believe she was spending the next couple of nights at overnight camp rather than at a hospital.

Maddie's return to Lurie's Place did not disappoint. To kick off her camp session, an organization was doing photo shoots during Maddie's pre-chemo screening appointment. And boy did she put on a show! We've never had professional pictures taken before, but Maddie could've fooled us. With every picture, her natural instinct was to do this cute little shoulder shrug, tilt her head to the side, and smile for the camera. If any one of us were about to start Mega Treatment III, wouldn't we be doing the same?

Maddie's day only grew better from there. She was reunited with her favorite nurse's assistant, Dani. Maddie played hospital bingo (literally, a hospital-wide bingo game with each floor participating via telecast). And who won you ask? None other than Grandma of course! Maddie was very impressed. Grandma told her that it was nothing and she should see her play Mahjong.

Maddie concluded her night walking around the 17th Floor and giving individual "Badges" (i.e., animal stickers) to all of the nurses for "being brave." It's hard to let cancer get you too down when Maddie is running the show.

Absent any setback, Maddie should be discharged from Lurie's Place on Thursday. We'll then try to enjoy the week or so before the F'n Ns take over. Until then, back to camp!

The Other Side of the (Mega Treatment) Mountain (7/14/17)

Maddie returned home this morning from her inpatient stay for Mega Treatment III. Just as her return to Shirley Ryan marked a moment of reflection, the view from the other side of the Mega Treatment Mountain is just as impressive. At this point, it's not just the vantage point of the Mega Treatments that's altered. We are altered.

On a moment's notice, I can look back at my former self on the former side of this mountain. Every painful scene is etched into my memory. Maddie's legs buckling under her on the scale in triage on April 20th. The Neurology Fellow incapable of getting the words out to describe what she saw on Maddie's MRI, and instead wrapping her hands around her neck to visually exhibit the location of the growth. Maddie laying helpless, unconscious, and intubated before being taken away for pre-op. Pacing the halls for the 6-plus hours of her surgery. Praying to see that smile just one more time. My first steps onto 17th Floor. The first chemo drip. The pain. The hurt. The darkness.

These snippets of sadness are all still at my fingertips. At the edge of my throat. Capable of a convulsive trigger with the right (or wrong) conversation.

But on the other side of the mountain, what's disappeared is the rawness. The helplessness. The feeling that the mountain of Cancer is bigger than us. And while the other side of the mountain may not be "all that we can see," it is primarily what we feel. We feel the momentum of our progress. We feel the gratitude for Maddie's progress. We feel the pride of being Maddie's parents.

That's not to say that the sadness is gone. Every single day is truly an immense blessing with an equally large asterisk hovering over it. Sometimes that asterisk brings tears. Sometimes it brings anger. Sometimes confusion. But in no case does it reach the all-consuming levels that came with our first steps onto the mountain.

Instead, we now just live with the sadness. Side by side with sadness as opposed to being subsumed by sadness. There's even an oddly inherent connection between that ever-present stream of sadness and the immense blessing I feel for every day. Almost as if you can't have one without the other.

Pammy said to me the other day, "You know, in many ways this is the most special time in our lives." What an insane statement. And yet, it's true. Here we are. Being choked by the sourest lemon that life has to offer. And at the same time, we are still capable of being consumed by the sweetness that is Maddie. The connection that Pammy and I each have with Maddie at this moment, and the intensity of the emotion flowing in all directions, is overpowering. And so unbelievably inspiring and fulfilling.

So as Maddie returns home tonight from Mega Treatment III and lays on her freshly-washed Minnie Mouse sheets, I am taking a moment to smile. Yes, I recognize that while we scale down this edge of the Mega Treatment Mountain there is undoubtedly another equally dramatic peak awaiting our battle-tested legs. But for today, I stand in awe of the view. And what more beautiful of a focal point than our sweet little Maddie. I love you, kiddo.

Maddie Medical Update (7/20/17)

Team Maddie,

No news is good news here. Since Maddie's Mega Treatment III last Tuesday, she's been in wonderful spirits. F'n Ns are supposed to hit within 7-10 days of the start of her treatment, so we're definitely on the clock. Whatever happens, it's been a wonderful run this round (poo poo poo, as Grandma would say). We'll keep you all posted on our return to Lurie's Place. In the meantime, Go Maddie Go.

Eyes on the Prize (7/21/17)

"Two more minutes, Daddy!" Maddie cries.

"But I'm not ready!" she exclaims.

Other than "Can we turn on Peppa?" these are probably two of the more common refrains at our house these days. The reason? Oral Meds.

Maddie currently has about 5 daily doses of oral medications. And because she's not pill-ready yet, we're typically rotating between a combination of syringe squirts and hidden applesauced tablets (lord knows when this year is over none of us will be able to even look at applesauce ever again). As you can imagine, getting a toddler to stop playing so that she can have something vile from the vial is not the easiest of tasks. Forget any divorce settlement meetings I've attended. The negotiation of Maddie vs. Medication is one for the ages. The kid drives a tough bargain.

But more than two months into this drill, we're starting to finally outsmart this three-foot negotiator. The art of our deal? The tag team combo of Stickers & Prizes. Scott & Pammy arriving at our own S&P Method. How does the S&P Method work?

Step 1: Take a medication.

Step 2: Get a sticker for the sticker chart (this being a prime negotiation, don't show up with just any sticker. You better bring your best Peppa, Dory, Frozen, Sesame, etc. to the table).
Step 3: Rinse and Repeat until the chart is full.
Step 4: Get a PRIZE!

Oh, you want two more minutes, Maddie? Not feeling ready for your medication? Well, do you want your *prize* tonight???

Done deal. Medicine never tasted finer.

By literally keeping Maddie's eyes on the prize every night, she's become a diligent (and slightly less resistant) medicine taker. 352 days of nightly prizes, we'll see how this turns out for Mommy and Daddy. But hey, we're playing the short game right now. Get through each night. With her eyes on the prize. If that means we need to hear 13-year-old Maddie saying, "Yo Pops, I ate my entire dinner, now where's my prize?" Well, I'd say if we get to that point we've all won this game.

Unfortunately, no amount of S&P Method was going to keep the F'n Ns stay at bay forever. Maddie returned to Lurie's Place today, as her temperature exceeded 100.5 on two occasions within an hour early this morning.

And while Mommy and Daddy leave the prizes behind when we go to Lurie's Place, Maddie keeps playing her own winning game. She doesn't know it, but every single day, whether at home or at Lurie's Place, Maddie is dropping daily doses of prizes that keep Pammy and me going. Every smile. Every hug. Every giggle. Every shimmy shake. Every nighttime song. Every good morning chit-chat.

Maddie is a walking prize.

Tonight, as the clock slowly inches past midnight, our prize-dropping negotiator sleeps peacefully. With a few new characters from the movie *Sing* scattered on her hospital bedside. Surrounded by her bedazzled room. Without a care in the world. Except maybe what the next prize will be when she gets home.

Lucky for Mommy and Daddy, that's about the only concern we don't have. Because we know that answer for us. We know what our prize is as parents. And we give thanks for her. Every single day.

Maddie Medical Update (7/22/17)

Team Maddie,

Maddie spent a perfect Saturday at Lurie's Place. Fever-free. And a fun-filled day with Grandpa, Grandma, Uncle Mikey Boy, and...Cinderella! Lurie's Place had a Superhero Hour, and the magical princess stopped by to say hi. She briefly confused Grandpa for Prince Charming. A common mistake. Iron Man was also in the building, but apparently Maddie wasn't really having any of that.

Her ANC should be zero for the next couple of days. So she's not out of the woods yet (typically other side effects join the party), but today was a pleasant surprise to say the least.

Easy Peasy Lemon Squeezy (7/23/17)

M addie has officially entered the toddler stage of "What does [insert word] mean?" If you read a book or watch a television show with Maddie these days, you'll inevitably get that exact question: "What does [insert word] mean?" It's an adorable and hilarious stage. And also shockingly difficult as a parent. You never would realize how hard it is to explain the meaning of even the most basic words until you're posed the question by a curious toddler. I smell a game show concept. Potentially a comeback opportunity for Jeff Foxworthy. But I digress.

This morning, Maddie and I were watching *Mickey Mouse Clubhouse* at Lurie's Place. Maddie's favorite character, Pete (yes, Pete is Maddie's favorite character), finished up some menial clubhouse task only to shout in that distinctive Pete voice (OK, so maybe 1 of 5 of you know how Pete sounds):

Easy peasy lemon squeezy!

Maddie and I both started laughing.

"What does easy peasy lemon squeezy mean?"

I'll tell you all what that means. *This F'n Ns stay.* At the risk of giving bulletin board material to Chemo, you heard me correctly. Easy. Peasy. Lemon. Squeezy. 3 days, 2 sleepless nights. And Maddie was officially discharged TODAY. I still can't believe it.

Post Mega 1: 12 days inpatient
Post Mega 2: 5 days inpatient
Post Mega 3: 3 days inpatient

3 days inpatient. Holy guacamole and easy peasy lemon squeezy!

It's not lost on me that only in this warped world can I call a 3-day inpatient hospital stay, where they wake you every three hours throughout the night, easy peasy lemon squeezy. But even crazier, in the twisted world of life A.C., this entire Mega III month has been pretty unbelievable.

Sure, the spectrum of awesomeness has certainly changed rapidly. Hospital stays, "baby pokes" (i.e., the Deputy Daddy subcutaneous shot), oral meds, daily nausea...this is the new baseline in the Kramer Household. If that's all you're talking, Chemo, bring it on! Because while in life B.C. any one of those things would possibly ruin our day, if not our month, that's now Maddie's norm. And she can dance and sing her way through any of these new normal occurrences. So in that warped way, Mega Treatment III has been a dream compared to previous experiences. Like sprinting through a torrential rainstorm with an enormous umbrella. We know it's pouring out there, but we don't feel much.

OK, so maybe that's a slightly long depiction of easy peasy lemon squeezy. But it's 9:35 p.m. on Sunday night. Prepared for a 5-7 day stay, I have a pile of unworn clothes resting in my suitcase. Yet for a brief and unexpected moment, I am able to physically and mentally unpack. Because we're home. Maddie's dancing. Maddie's bathing. Maddie's oral medsing. Maddie's baby poking. Maddie's TPNing. Maddie's reading. Maddie's bedside concerting.

And Maddie's sleeping. With Minnie on her covers. And Peppa by her side.

Easy peasy lemon squeezy.

Maddie Update (7/31/17)

Move over, Anthony Rizzo. That chance meeting may have blown away Mommy, Daddy, Family, and Friends. But in Maddie's World, the encounter she had today will stay with her for quite some time. Maddie came face to face with...

The Penguins!

No, not the Pittsburgh Penguins. The Lincoln Park Zoo Penguins! Special thanks to Uncle Steve and Aunt Nanci for making this amazing Meet and Greet possible. Maddie's behind-the-scenes tour of the penguin exhibit couldn't have been cooler. She saw their kitchen, their playroom, their bedrooms, and the grand finale – a face-to-face encounter *inside the exhibit itself.*

The timing couldn't have been more perfect. Maddie is operating at 100%. She's full of life, smiles, and even some renewed pudge in those cheeks. With Mega Treatment IV on tap for Wednesday pending medical clearance, we're soaking up these Independence Days. And Maddie clearly is too. She went Napless in Chicago only to crash mid-bedtime story, each of which is a rare occurrence these days. Buy hey, mucking it up with the penguins is hard work. See you soon, penguins!

Don't Stop Believin' (8/1/17)

Seven years ago today, Pammy and I circled one
another seven times before entering the warmth of a
shared *tallis* under a sheltering *chuppah*. Following our
wedding ceremony, we stepped onto the Temple Beth
Sholom dance floor together surrounded by our closest
family and friends. After the band announced the entrance
of Mr. and Mrs. Kramer for the first time, they jumped right
into our First Dance song...

Journey's *Don't Stop Believin'*.

If Pammy and I were to each list out places where we
felt most comfortable, I can safely say that the dance floor
wouldn't have cracked the top ten. But there we were, our
family and friends cheering us on, as we dutifully tracked
our pre-wedding ballroom dancing instructions through this
classic '80s rock anthem. Step by step. Dancing our way into
marriage.

In some ways, the beginning of our married life is just
the yin to the yang we now face. But the Journey we're on
now is *our* Journey. And while Pammy and I are in the
middle of this A.C. dance floor, there's a new, cuter star of
the unwelcomed show dancing her way through. Our family
and friends are still surrounding us. Willing us to keep going.

Enveloping us with the same love and support albeit on a much colder floor.

But the theme is the same. We are taking this Journey step by step. Move by move. And the chorus has never been packed with more meaning.

Don't Stop Believin'.

I'll say it again.

Don't Stop Believin'.

With Maddie by our side (or more accurately, with Maddie leading the way with unparalleled strength), we will not stop believing. We will not fade to black. We will hold on to that feeling.

That feeling that anything is possible. That feeling that a two-and-a-half-year-old girl can have her life flipped upside down. Lose her ability to so much as stand. And yet come out the other side dancing like nobody's watching. That feeling that two parents, who met randomly as seniors at the Brown Jug in Ann Arbor, Michigan, could crumble into each other's arms in an MRI waiting room only to rise as one and hold each other up again. To become the strongest parents for the strongest little girl. That feeling of fostering a loving home. That feeling of building a family. That feeling of being Team Maddie.

When you take your vows, in sickness and in health, no one pictures this moment. No one can prepare you for this challenge. But here we are. And I couldn't have a more perfect dance partner in Pammy. While I may be the voice for you all into our Journey, Pammy is the one who is really leading the way. She is Maddie's guide. Her maestro. Her rock.

And I am a blessed husband.

August 1, 2010. To August 1, 2017. Seven circles. To seven years. Happy Anniversary, Pammy. Don't stop believin'...

Maddie Medical Update (8/3/17)

Team Maddie,

Maddie's streak of chemo delays is alive and well. Maddie was scheduled initially to begin Mega Treatment IV yesterday morning. Unfortunately, her counts were too low to proceed. So much for the free night's stay (yay for out-of-pocket maximums!) at Lurie's Place for our anniversary celebration. I think Maddie is just trying to boost the ratings for Mega IV.

In the meantime, we're hoping for a nice week to rest Maddie's bones before she steps back in the ring next Tuesday. We'll keep you all posted. Thank you for all of the positive thoughts this week!

Maddie Medical Update II (8/3/17)

Team Maddie,

I realized that I neglected to say...Maddie is doing awesome! Even though her counts are down, she's on top of her game. Hopefully more of the same during this delay of game period.

Maddie Medical Update (8/8/17)

Team Maddie,

Looks like another delay of game today. Maddie's counts are still lagging a bit for treatment this week. But she's not concerned. Maddie has Mommy by her side and a replacement patient in Lily for all of her imaginative doctor-patient play (since we have met our deductible for the year, Lily has consented to all exams and treatments from Dr. Maddie). We'll give Mega IV another whirl next Tuesday. Here's to another great week!

Maddie Medical Update (8/11/17)

Team Maddie,

It's been an eventful 24 hours in the Kramer Household. The action started at 3:00 a.m. with Maddie sitting up in her bed. She's chatting away. Something is off. Pammy takes her temperature. The result? 100.5. Which means we have to take her temperature again an hour later to see if she still hits 100.5. Pammy and I start to pack our things for the hospital figuring the inevitable fever is coming. About two minutes into the hour that we're required to wait, Lily starts screaming.

[Insert Expletive].

Ah, the joys of parenthood!

Pammy's now taking care of Lily. I'm packing up our hospital gear and monitoring Maddie. 4:00 a.m. comes. No fever. Call off the ER dogs for now. But then 4 hours, more Lily screams, and no sleep later, Maddie has a fever again. 100.5. By 9:30 a.m., it's off to the ER. Are we having fun yet?

Fortunately, there's a positive end to this story. Every time Maddie's fever spiked, she seemed to keep fighting it off. To the point where the doctors concluded that she was able to go home for the time being. Come 7:00 p.m., what does no sleep and an emergency room stay look like? Maddie racing around our living room singing and dancing to *Get Back Up Again* from the *Trolls* movie. A perfect theme song for our resilient hero. That's Maddie for you.

The Miracle of Lily (8/13/17)

In these pages and pages of writings, there's an untold story. An untold story who goes by the name of Lily. A fitting name for our little bright flower born briefly before this unspeakable storm.

Lily came into this world on February 13, 2017. Just two months B.C. The timing of her birth continues to astound me. Arriving in this beautiful and narrow window of life that allowed us to bask in her newborn sunshine.

Imagine if Lily were born just a bit later. The thought of Pammy being mid-pregnancy while coping with Maddie's diagnosis. The thought of Pammy being in the hospital at the same time as Maddie.

I've also imagined if Pammy had not yet become pregnant. It's safe to say that having another child wouldn't exactly be on our to do list at the moment.

For Pammy and me, the timing of Lily's birth, in my heart of hearts, is another miracle to celebrate. Another positive place to point when posited the ever-present, "Why Us?"

While Lily arrived with a whimper on February 13th, the moment she came home from the hospital, that whimper quickly crashed into a bone-chilling scream. I can still picture the look on our night nurse's face the evening we parted ways (yes, Lily drove away a *paid* night nurse who had been allegedly baby whispering for decades). The woman looked up at me, sleep deprived and defeated, in her deep Jamaican voice: "I don't know what da hell to do with dis baby!"

Welcome to the world, Lily.

Looking back, I sometimes wonder if Lily knew what was coming. If she was trying to tell us something. Bellowing the pain we'd all soon feel. I still vividly remember chatting with Pammy during our sleepless B.C. nightshifts, as we'd try to motivate one another to wake up and calm Lily's colicky crying chorus. "May this be the worst thing we have to experience," we'd say.

Unfortunately, Lily's screams didn't lie. Before we could even wipe the newborn glow off our faces (or wash away the newborn bags under our eyes), before Maddie could even adjust to what it meant to be a big sister, we echoed Lily's painful cries from an MRI waiting room.

And yet just as miraculous, no sooner did we get through Maddie's miraculous recovery from surgery than did Lily become the calmest, smiliest, happiest, and yes even nighttime sleepiest, baby on the block. As if we hadn't already entered the twilight zone, Lily went from her nightly reenactment of *The Exorcist* to a welcomed portrayal of *Sleeping Beauty*.

I'm convinced that Lily's transformation was not a coincidence. That Lily is here for a reason. That Lily is our untold miracle. While I still haven't ruled out an alternate genetic source for this blond-haired blue-eyed bundle of baby rolls, she is undoubtedly a product of love. Without exaggeration, Lily is a literal smile machine. A human doll skilled at mirroring back the love thrown her way. If you look at Lily and so much as grin, you'll immediately get back a full-blown chubby-cheeked, open-mouth smile that – for one brief second – makes you forget every ounce of sorrow in this A.C. World.

Coincidence or not, we are blessed for Lily's presence. We are blessed for her perpetual joy. Because no matter how difficult any particular moment might be, we can't resist that smile. It's the smile of innocence. The smile of joy. The smile of hope. The smile of another miracle keeping her family moving forward.

Lillian Zelda, never underestimate your role in this journey. Even when we couldn't be there for you, you were there for us. Plus, I hear the brightest flowers love a good rainstorm. And words can't do justice to your exuberance. Happy Six Month Birthday, Lily Bug.

Maddie Medical Update (8/15/17)

Team Maddie,

After two consecutive false starts, Maddie is officially cleared to begin Mega Treatment IV today. Please send positive vibes and prayers her way. To no one's surprise, Maddie is chatting up all of the nurses on the clinic floor and "working" away on the in-room computer. The 17th Floor (and most importantly, the playroom) await...

What's Next? (8/17/17)

Attention span has never quite been Maddie's strongest trait. To this day, one of my favorite memories of Maddie is her time in music class. B.C., Pammy and I enrolled Maddie in music class up to three days per week. Partly because she loved it. And partly because it was just something to break up the day (don't be ashamed to admit it, parents).

While Maddie loved these classes, let's just say sitting patiently and clapping calmly to the beat wasn't her jam. Instead, the more common scene would be a room full of children sitting nicely in a circle and clapping and singing along with the teacher, and a little, curly-haired girl running in circles around the circle as fast as she could.

Maddie never stopped moving. In music and in life, her mind and body just kept going. And so a few minutes into these thirty-minute classes, or frankly any activity between the ages of 12-24 months, Maddie's most common mid-activity refrain would be:

"What's Next?"

I can still hear her in my head. It cracked me up each time. Except maybe when the invoice came for 12 thirty-minute music sessions of which Maddie maybe focused for

5 minutes per session. As Mega Treatment IV now comes to a close, we find ourselves asking the same question:

"What's Next?"

Make no mistake, we still have a very long treatment road ahead. This journey is far from over. Altogether, Maddie has 13 inpatient chemo cycles remaining over the next 42 weeks (assuming no delays), and we don't expect any to be cake walks. So, you ask, what made the Megas mega? Why the build up? What have we all been rooting for this entire time?

Undoubtedly, there are still Mega benefits that come with putting Mega IV in our rearview mirror. For one, there are two chemo drugs, one of which is particularly brutal from a side effect perspective, that Maddie is not scheduled to see ever again. Sayonara, Cisplatin! You will not be missed. Do not expect a thank you card.

Just as exciting, starting in three weeks, Maddie no longer has to visit Lurie's Place for "mini treatments" every week. Instead, she'll be limited to tri-weekly chemo treatments.

But in truth, I think the Mega-ist benefit of moving on from Mega IV is our collective metamorphosis that has progressed with each stay. Looking back at my writings from 45-60 days ago, it's like reading the words of a former self. The pain was so palpable. Each chapter written with equal parts hurt and love with a pinch of hope. With Mega IV behind us, I now write with an added ingredient. An ingredient that I've felt building with each day:

Acceptance.

To be honest, I'm slowly realizing that this mentality shift was the biggest reason that the doctors focused on these first four Mega Treatments. As I've said before, you have to break it down to avoid breaking down. And that's what the doctors did for us by focusing on these first four treatments. They broke it down. Because the bigger picture of life A.C., and Maddie's treatment course, is unimaginably daunting. If we spent every morning dwelling on the volume of challenges we have remaining, we wouldn't be able to make it to noon. The amount of hospital stays is still too numerous to count. Nausea and needle-filled nights appear endless. And of course, The Great Unknown for what the ultimate future looks like is always hovering.

You have to break it down to avoid breaking down. And that's why we have Maddie. Our Mini Monk on this marathon we're marching through. Reminding us that there's only one question today. Only one question right now.

What's *Next?*

What's immediately *next?*

And next to me as I contemplate what's next is still the cutest, most precious girl I know. Clutching a little Baloo character that she borrowed from the 17th Floor Playroom. What's next is we get to go home together today. What's next is we get to celebrate the major accomplishment of powering through these first four Mega Treatments. Of seeing Maddie transition from Fear to Fantastic. What's next is we get to sleep in our own beds. What's next is we get to hang with Lily Poo. What's next is we get to play in our own playroom for the next 7-10 days. What's next is we get to continue to watch in awe of Maddie's strength.

Just like her days in music class, what's next is that Maddie keeps moving. Only with a Mega notch under her belt.

PART SIX

Maddie and the Amazing Half-Inch (8/22/16)

Today was a day of growth. We arrived at Lurie's Place this morning for Maddie's second to last weekly chemo treatment (quick, weekly "pushes" of chemo into her central line). After next week, she'll receive treatment every three weeks or so. We knew this coming into today. What we didn't know was that there was some "bigger" news in store. Maddie entered the clinic floor...wait for it...a half an inch taller.

I know what you're thinking. A half an inch? Call off The Guinness Book of World Records press conference. But hey, height doesn't exactly grow on this vertically challenged branch of the family tree, so celebrate we will. Just as exciting, it's the first sign of physical growth for Maddie since she started chemo. After stalling at three foot nothing for months, Maddie sported this surprise half-inch boost during her pre-chemo screening. Chemo *literally* can't keep Maddie down.

The development packed into that half-inch is almost unthinkable. In a matter of months, Maddie has experienced more trauma and challenge than most of us ever will in our entire lives. Today was another reminder of how far Maddie has come since we first set foot in the hospital. The contrast is black and white. And that contrast came to a complete head (or more accurately, a spine and a head), as Maddie and

I strolled past the hallway meeting room on the Lurie's Place outpatient clinic floor. While walking by, I couldn't help but notice a black-and-white image magnified on the projection screen (clearly the subject of some previous medical team meeting). I would know that image anywhere. I hadn't seen it live since the early hours of April 21st, but it's etched into my memory. Carved into my heart. There was no mistaking the picture. The familiar outline of a skull. The slightly curved spine. With a grey blob embedded in the spinal cord.

I reacted quickly and positively: "Look Maddie, it's your X-ray!" I said (Doc McStuffins hasn't covered MRIs yet). She stared in amazement. As did I. Just for obviously different reasons. On April 21st, I feared that black-and-white picture might be the last I saw of Maddie. That all of her brightness would be reduced to that god-awful photo. And yet here we were, April 21st Maddie and August 22nd Maddie face to face. Only one of these faces was now a half an inch taller. And smiling brightly back at the digital memory of her former self.

That says it all, doesn't it? A picture worth well more than a thousand words. Because thankfully August 22nd Maddie is not just a picture. She's a daughter. A sister. A granddaughter. A niece. A cousin. A friend. A hero. A miracle.

Our miracle.

There is nothing black and white about this little girl except maybe her exuberance. Just ask the Lurie staff. As all other patients wait quietly in their rooms for the doctor, there's one three-foot-and-a-half-an-inch toddler bouncing around the hallways. She's pointing out the different animal pictures on the wall. She's waving to all of the nurses. She's dancing to Beatles songs streaming on the iPad. She's requesting the "pink house" from the playroom. She's doing her "work" on the nursing station computer. She's reminding everyone that she's on the "Kitty Floor" (yes, it turns out there is a picture of a kitty near the elevators). Most importantly, four months later, from April 21st to August 22nd, she's still smiling. She's still growing. She's still being Maddie.

A half an inch never felt so huge.

Maddie Medical Update (8/26/17)

Team Maddie,

Quite a day for our little rock star. Maddie's day kicked off midmorning with an appointment for a transfusion at Lurie's Place. 7 hours later, all transfusions were complete. Yes, 7 hours. For those keeping score at home, Mommy was the unanimous MVP today.

Post-transfusion, we were minutes from going home. And of course, at 6:30 p.m., what happens? 101 degree temp. You know what that means. F'n Ns!

No skin off Maddie's back. It's throwback Friday, as they sent us to the 19th floor for our overnight visit (the neurosurgery floor where Maddie first stayed post-surgery back in April). Better yet, the nurses here lined her bed with toys upon arrival.

Good news, by late tonight, Maddie's fever was already down, and she was in great spirits all day. Please pray for a quick recovery!

In the meantime, Maddie is sleeping away with her new pal "Bananas" by her side (a Beanie Boo monkey from the nurses). Sweet dreams, Maddie.

Soup and Two Surprises (8/27/17)

I drove back to Lurie's Place today around 4:30 p.m. After spending the day with Lily, I headed back for the evening swap with Pammy. Pammy and I are chatting on the phone during my drive down Lake Shore. I can hear Maddie in the background ordering her dinner.

"Mommy, I'll have soup and two surprises!"

Soup and two surprises.

That might not seem like much to you at first glance. But four months ago, Maddie was not an *any surprises* kind of girl. From my earlier writings, you may recall that one of the biggest hurdles we envisioned for Maddie was learning to adjust to the constant chaos that comes with cancer. The same child who loved starting her morning listing out what day it was, who was coming, and what we would be doing, was forced into a world where unpredictability reigned supreme. And tonight, the former Queen of Consistency donned her newfound Crown of Chaos. Or shall I say, she swallowed it down in spoonfuls of soul warming soup with her two surprise sides of cantaloupe and green beans.

This didn't happen over the course of one dinner. Slowly, during the last couple of months, when Pammy would prepare Maddie for the day ahead, Pammy started introducing a new concept. Something so simple yet so complex for a young mind. The concept? Two words:

"We'll see…"

Watching Maddie learn to understand these two words, and embrace the future unknown embodied in their meaning, has been amazing. And without question, the idea of introducing this mantra of malleability was all Mommy. Surely this was not a discourse decided by a Daddy who digs peanut butter sandwiches day in and day out. Instead, I heard the finished product of Pammy's lessons firsthand.

"Daddy, we're going to go to Lurie's Place, they'll check my vitamins, and then maybe we'll sleep over. *We'll see…*"

"Daddy, tomorrow we'll go to the playroom and then after maybe we'll go home. *We'll see…*"

What an amazing concept for a three-year-old child to embrace, especially one originally raised on a steady diet of consistency and predictability. No crying about when we'll go home. No longing for getting out of Lurie's Place. No stressing about the uncertainties of each day. Just being at peace with "we'll see."

And yet again, we all have something to learn from Maddie. You all know my M.O. at this point. Deputy Daddy. Mr. Peanut Butter Sandwich. Habit and routine is always my dream. Chaos my kryptonite. But let's face it, we are living in one big mess of We'll See right now. We don't know what tomorrow will bring, let alone what post-chemo life has in store. Accepting We'll See, and being at peace with We'll See, is the only course to conquering the chaos that is cancer.

Embrace We'll See. Be We'll See. Be like Maddie. I think I'm on to a new morning meditative prayer. I have no doubt

I'll never be as successful in this transition as my three-year-old hero. But I can try and start with my next lunch order. Perhaps a peanut butter sandwich and two surprises? We'll see...

Maddie Medical Update (8/28/17)

Team Maddie,

Well, Maddie has done it again. We were home in less than 48 hours, which is the minimum admission for an F'n Ns stay. Even after only two nights away, there's nothing like coming home. Maddie's infection-fighting counts are still pretty low, so we hope for an uneventful week back at the ranch (with Maddie's final weekly chemotherapy treatment scheduled for Tuesday and continuing every three weeks after that). Maddie was in great spirits, and she fell asleep tonight with ease. Way to fight and play your way through another round, kiddo!

Maddie Medical Update (9/3/17)

Team Maddie,

Hail to this little victor! Maddie's post F'n Ns run has been a total success. 7 straight days of feeling good all peaking in time for Michigan's opening day kickoff yesterday. Even Maddie couldn't resist the excitement of those All Maize unis! Although, she made one thing very clear:

"Daddy, after your show we get to watch my shows. Deal?"

Hard to argue with that kind of offer. One Maize & Blue "W" later, we traded in our Wolverines for some *Goldie & Bear*. I could've endured a whole season of G&B after that kind of dominant gridiron showing.

Quite a weekend for Maddie on top of it. Zoo Time, multiple ice cream runs, first night sans baby poke tonight (after 14 straight days at home with an evening injection), Toys "R" Us, aquarium...we are pulling out all the local stops while we can. Counts permitting, Maddie's next treatment is scheduled for Tuesday. Until then, one more day of Zoo Time and Ice Cream await.

Maddie Medical Update (9/5/17)

Team Maddie,

Maddie was the ultimate trooper today. We hit the road at 8:15 a.m. for Lurie's Place. While Maddie wasn't cleared for a full treatment round (her counts were too low today; they'll check again on Thursday), she proceeded with her lumbar puncture (where the chemo is injected into the fluid surrounding her spinal cord). The procedure is extremely quick but requires anesthesia, so the day itself is still pretty long and draining.

After waiting four hours for the procedure to begin, and then getting knocked out from the anesthesia for another two hours, Maddie awoke with a smile on her face and a simple question:

"Daddy, can we watch *Hey Duggee*?" (The obscure Nick Jr. show she was watching two hours before the anesthesia kicked in.)

You would have thought she was waking up from any ordinary nap. As if the hospital and nursing staff were just background noise. Not that I should be surprised at this point. Our little hero always seems up for the challenge. Six hours and a surprise Sweet Mandy B's cupcake run later,

Maddie is fast asleep. Probably hoping *Hey Duggee* is on when she comes out of this slumber too...

Maddie Medical Update (9/7/17)

Team Maddie,

Not exactly to our surprise, Maddie's treatment today was delayed again until next Wednesday (counts permitting). For those keeping score at home, Maddie historically has needed an extra week or two after each cycle for her counts to fully recover for the next go-around. Although you certainly wouldn't know it by looking at her. She's been in fantastic spirits, and we're all just trying to enjoy the extra time at home. Besides, she really didn't want to watch the Michigan game this weekend from a Lurie's Place bed. That's really what this is all about.

Please keep the prayers coming.

We Are Aware (9/12/17)

September is Childhood Cancer Awareness Month. I can tell you what my awareness would have looked like in September 2016 B.C. One year ago, I may have noticed when a White Sox player donned yellow wristbands to honor the occasion. Or perhaps catch a moving Facebook post. That would have been the extent of my awareness, and I would have gone on with my day-to-day routines. In September 2017, awareness is the least of my issues. I am all too aware. Every month is cancer awareness month. Every day. Every hour. Every minute.

I am now acutely aware of the absolute crippling characteristics of childhood cancer. I am aware of what it is like for your life to change in the blink of an eye (or worse yet, a collapse on a triage scale). I am aware of how it feels to spend six straight hours pacing without pause on a hospital waiting room floor not knowing if I would ever hear the sweetest voice in the world again. I am aware of the debilitating pain. I am aware of the darkest of fears. I am aware of the helplessness.

But I am also aware of resilience. I am aware of the strength of the human spirit. I am aware of the gift of innocence. I am aware of the power of imagination. I am aware of what it means to take every ounce of pain that could be pummeling your pounding heart and instead propelling that pain into positive purpose. I am aware of feeling blessed in a time when you may otherwise be tempted to curse the world. I am aware of all-consuming love. I am aware of hope. I am aware of daily miracles.

And perhaps most importantly in this Childhood Cancer Awareness Month, I am aware that we are not alone. While Maddie's experience may be – with limited exceptions – our only glimpse into the world of childhood cancer, this is sadly not a story just for me to tell. We do not have a monopoly on pain. We do not have exclusive rights to hope. The beds at Lurie's Place are literally overflowing with pediatric cancer patients. And that same scene is playing out across the country. Each and every one of these families has a story to tell. Their triage moment. Their inspirations. Their blessings. I am aware that we are nothing more than a window into that world. And that we are blessed with a daughter whose unparalleled spirit offers a glimpse into every reason to stay aware of childhood cancer. She is Miracle Maddie. The girl who jokes through the baby pokes. The girl who smiles through the medicine vials. The girl who is dancing while cancering.

And while I know at this point you are all aware of Maddie, and you are aware of our journey, please also be aware of what a precious piece you are in the childhood cancer puzzle. Be aware that you have made – and you can continue to make – a difference. Be aware that you don't need to suffer in order to support. Be aware that being a supportive friend, co-worker, family member, or even stranger is one of the biggest blessings you have provided us on this journey. Whether in a text message, a donation, a meal, a phone call, a gift, a card, a visit, a private evening prayer, or even just keeping up with Maddie's journey, we are aware of what a difference you've each made in our lives.

We are aware of you. We are aware of gratitude. And we are aware of the transformative power of remaining aware.

Maddie Medical Update (9/13/17)

Team Maddie,

Maddie's counts are still making their way back to baseline, so she won't proceed with chemo today. She'll get checked again on Friday to see if she's ready to roll with the next round. Fortunately, this delay has provided Maddie with extra time to bulk up for the big day. She's been eating better than she ever has in this process. Hopefully that will bring a little extra strength come game time.

Maddie Medical Update (9/15/17)

Team Maddie,

Apparently good sleep and a few Oreos go a long way. Maddie officially has been given the green light for Round V. Her counts are high, and her weight is up around two full pounds in the last week. Go Maddie Go!

She's going to need every bit of gain. This round consists of five consecutive days of chemo running on an ongoing, 24-hour basis. The primary enemy? Doxo be thy name. Historically, Doxo has been rough on her immune system and shelled out the dreaded mouth sores, so we will be saying our prayers extra hard this time around.

Here's to a quick five-day stay (how's that for an oxymoron), and an even quicker recovery period. And more importantly, here's to our almost 30-pound hero staying strong.

The Narrative (9/17/17)

I remember our first conversations with Maddie post-surgery. Our protective parental instincts kicked in immediately.

"Maddie, everything is going to be OK. The doctors are going to make everything feel better."

No detail. No explanation. Just unbridled positivity. There wasn't much else to say. This was our two-and-a-half-year-old baby girl. Our conversations centered around cartoons, the zoo, and swimming class. Hospitals, MRIs, and cancer didn't have a page in our family dictionary. So we started where most parents would in our situation. Preserve and protect.

Only our parental instincts were wrong. Or at least incomplete. Thankfully, one of the first professionals with whom we consulted at Lurie's Place was a child life specialist on the ICU floor. While I can't remember her name, or even picture her face (or anything else from that day except the vision of an intubated Maddie and the MRI image), I remember vividly how that conversation forever changed our lives. I am grateful for her impact on us as parents, but more importantly, for how she single-handedly and positively altered our course of keeping Maddie as Maddie.

Our guide told us, first and foremost, we must tell Maddie the truth. The truth? I think Jack Nicholson probably had the appropriate line for how we all felt about the truth at that moment. How could a child possibly endure any more, conversation or otherwise, after such a living nightmare?

But we took her lead. She explained that if we were to just tell Maddie that "everything is going to be OK" without further detail, we would be doing her a disservice. Our words needed to match her experience. Our words were the foundation for her understanding of this new upside down world around her as well as the stability of our parent-child relationship. For her to trust us, our words needed to resonate. She needed to make sense of the days and experiences ahead. The pain. The inability to walk. The poking. The prodding. The chemo. The doctors. We had to give her a framework.

So that's what we did. We abandoned our protective parental instincts. And we began working on a narrative to help Maddie understand her A.C. World. The Narrative started simple.

"Maddie, you know how your neck and back have been hurting very badly the past few days? Well, it turns out you had a little ball in your neck. The ball was called a 'tumor.' That was causing your pain. But guess what? Your super doctors took the tumor out!"

"Maddie, next we get to go to a cool place called Shirley Ryan. They're going to help you get stronger and walk better again. Because the tumor was so big it made it hard to walk."

"We get to go to Lurie's Place! They're going to give you a special medicine, called chemo, so that the tumor does not come back."

"You won't believe it, I think you're going to get a room with a TV! And they have a playroom!"

And so it went. With each passing week, the experiences changed, but the explanatory pattern repeated. Tell the truth but break it down into understandable concepts. We slowly grew to realize the immense power we had over the way Maddie would view her new A.C. World. Our word choice, and The Narrative, were our primary tools to shape that lens.

In doing so, we had a simple, underlying choice: resist or embrace. Pammy and I chose to embrace with unimaginable consistency.

To top it off, we added our own special ingredient – keeping The Narrative as positive and fun as reality would permit. After all, Lurie Children's Hospital is not a hospital where we visit reluctantly. This is "Lurie's Place" and it is *awesome!* We get excited about our car rides to Lurie's Place. We talk about who and what we'll see on each floor (are we going to the Kitty Floor or the Gorilla Floor?). We create silly songs for each medicine. We gush about the playroom. We don't pout about the chemo. We instead emphasize how the chemo is going to make us *stronger* and make sure that the tumor *does not come back*.

Fast forward nearly five months later. A full day of Lurie's Place fun with her family. Playroom. Dance parties. TV. Characters. Walks. I spy. Sleepovers. Because of The Narrative, Maddie is living through Lurie not living to leave Lurie.

The impact of The Narrative hit me especially hard last night. Our first night back for an inpatient chemo stay in quite some time. Maddie is playing on the guest couch. She turns to me and says,

"Daddy, let's pretend we're in a hospital [*cough cough*]. I'm sick [*cough cough*]. Daddy, you be the doctor," as she giggles through each cough.

The irony was palpable. Here she is, inpatient being treated for one of the harshest diseases life can throw at a human being, and Maddie is cheerfully "pretending" to be sick while unable to hold back the smiles.

Because five months later, Maddie is not "sick." The Narrative does not require her to be sick. Being sick is a mentality that offers her no utility. Instead, she gets chemo so that the tumor does not come back. Period. But that doesn't mean the rest of the world around her can't be immensely enjoyable otherwise.

The Narrative reminds us that we must ignore the emotional baggage that comes with being sick. That we must ward off the what-ifs. That we must forget the fears. The Narrative only requires this:

The truth. Broken down. With a personalized dash of fun.

Quite a recipe.

Maddie Medical Update (9/20/17)

Team Maddie,

Four nights and five days later, we are all at home again together after Round V. Maddie was absolutely amazing for this entire chemo stay at Lurie's Place. She maintained her spirit, playfulness, and energy level throughout.

No sooner did we turn onto Lake Shore Drive than did Maddie fall asleep. Going 110% every day (not to mention the impact of the chemo) had to catch up with her eventually. Through it all, Maddie is just such a light. And per usual, I leave these stays in absolute awe. She is my hero.

For now, we hope to enjoy a few quiet days at home and pray for the side effects to be as kind as possible. Sweet dreams, Maddie.

Our Book of Life (9/24/17)

We are in the midst of the Jewish New Year. Year 5778 in the Jewish Calendar. 5778 years. That's about the amount of time I feel has passed between April 21, 2017 and today.

One of the aspects of Judaism that I've always appreciated is the ease of secular adaptation. Even for those who are either not Jewish or not particularly religious, most Jewish holidays, prayers, and customs have a practical application that's easily digestible. The New Year has always been one of those holidays for me.

At its core, the New Year is about introspection and self-reflection. Take stock of the year passed and the year ahead. What did I do wrong? Who did I wrong? What did I do right? Who did I do right by? To me, the New Year was always my annual moment of zen. Reset and refresh. And the synagogue offered a quiet, focused venue for that process.

This year is a bit different. OK, so that's an understatement. But as you know from these pages and pages, I haven't exactly stored up much in the way of remaining moments of self-reflection for the New Year. Every waking moment since April 2017 has been a moment of self-reflection. Every waking moment in some ways a living prayer. That doesn't mean, however, that the holiday is somehow devoid of meaning. I'm just discovering new ways to apply it.

One of the primary biblical concepts this time of year is the Book of Life. The idea is that, on Rosh Hashanah (the beginning of the New Year), an almighty God begins making the sole determination of *Who Shall Live and Who Shall Die*. And that on Yom Kippur, the bookend holiday that follows a week after Rosh Hashanah to conclude this period of reflection, that same almighty God finalizes that determination.

On Rosh Hashanah it is written, and on Yom Kippur it is sealed.

On account of Maddie's condition, I didn't attend synagogue for the New Year this year. I didn't have my formal moment of religion-inspired zen. But I know this – I don't know how I would've handled hearing those italicized words. I'm not quite sure that, even if just a biblical metaphor, I could grapple with Maddie's fate being predetermined at this exact moment in time. To feel that the next seven days, from Rosh Hashanah to Yom Kippur, carry the weight of the conclusion to her story.

So I've chosen a different application of the metaphor this year. And I realized we've been doing it since April 21st. The application is this:

We are writing our own Book of Life.

5 months and 80-plus Maddie's Miracles entries later, we are writing our own story. When we started tracking Maddie's story online, the opening forms asked us to inscribe a purpose for our writings. We did: "This site is committed to cherishing the little miracles that each day of Maddie's recovery brings." I don't even notice it on the top of the site anymore. It's just become a part of who we are.

From Day One, Pammy and I had a choice. Who shall live and who shall die? Put aside the literal meaning. Consider these words as a choice of how to approach life A.C. – through darkness or light. Through longing or living. Through a lens of death or a lens of life.

We Chose Life.

We chose to make this a year to *live* not a year to complete. A year to focus on *love* even if pain was always sitting right at the edge of our sleeve. A year to create *joy* in places where you would expect to find sadness. In creating The Narrative for Maddie, we created our narrative as well. Our very own Book of Life.

What a book it has been. While we all cannot wait to turn the page on chemo, on side effects, and on cancer, we can't just live for turning to the next page. We instead live for each word. Each smile. Each kiss. Each shimmy shake. Each carousel ride. Each goodnight song.

This is our life. This is our purpose. This is our book to write. None of us know what the last chapter of this story holds. But Pammy and I have taken on our role of authorship. And we feel blessed for each and every chapter.

Maddie Medical Update (9/29/17)

Team Maddie,

Grandma Sue's text message this evening said it best:

Holy ****

No, she wasn't referring to the Holy Days. Instead, now 13 days since Round V began, Maddie is still dancing...still smiling...still home. You read that correctly. We're still home.

Pammy and I have had our suitcases packed for Lurie's Place since last Saturday. Every night this week, we look at each other with an unmistakable expression that says..."Really?" Every morning this week, I walk into Maddie's room, wondering if this is the day where I feel that burning hot forehead. Instead, I just get a sweet voice and a cool *keppy*.

Five straight days of chemo. No nausea. No mouth sores. No fevers. No hospital stays.

Just Maddie.

I have no idea what's happening. And I know it can change in the blink of an eye. But for today, with Maddie's doctors confirming that her blood counts are on their way up faster than ever, we go to sleep thankful. You are one tough cookie, Maddie Kramer.

The View From 20,000...ANC (10/5/17)

What a way to cap off a treatment round. In many ways, the medical conclusion to a treatment round is the day when we can stop the "baby poke" (our nightly subcutaneous shot to boost Maddie's ANC). At the very least, it's our emotional conclusion to each round. We are only given clearance to stop the baby poke when Maddie's ANC reaches a certain acceptable level determined by the doctors. Overall, the goal is to boost her ANC numbers to fight infection sufficiently while also hoping that – when the numbers drop precipitously upon ceasing the baby poke – they at least remain high enough to permit Maddie to move forward with her next treatment round.

With the Medical Mumbo Jumbo moved to the side, here's the takeaway – after 14 straight nights of having to end an otherwise peaceful nighttime routine with an injection into Maddie's upper leg, the baby poke (and therefore this round) has come to an end. Yes, when Maddie laid her head down last night, the only sound I was blessed with hearing was this:

"Can you sing one more song, Daddy?"

(Gosh, those words get me every time.)

Just as exciting, the end to Round V brought a wonderful surprise, as Maddie's ANC was higher than it has ever been during this entire process: 20,000. And her rise couldn't feel more glorious.

This number, and frankly this round, signifies far more than just checking another round off this seemingly endless treatment protocol. 20,000 represents strength. 20,000 represents endurance. 20,000 represents triumph. 20,000 represents life. Because the side effects that we accepted as inevitable were nowhere to be found. You know the list at this point. The mouth sores. The excruciating pain. The constant vomiting. The fevers. The hospital stays. While any number of these setbacks could hit at any time, we can at least look ahead knowing that anything really is possible.

Not that we should need a reminder at this point. Maddie pretty much embodies this reality every day. If it weren't for her cute little bald head, you really wouldn't know anything materially harmful is going on inside her body. She is, in every single way, her beautiful self. And I will never underestimate the beauty of that fact.

Consider this – as Round V comes to a close, we have been living A.C. life for more than five months now. More than 150 days. Approximately 1/8 of Maddie's entire life. But Cancer has not overtaken her life. Chemo has not overtaken her life. They have just become absorbed into her even more powerful and infectious smile.

As we sit atop this view from 20,000 ANC, Pammy and I have no idea what awaits in any one of the next 12 rounds. But we've learned there's a new amazing gift in that unknown:

A renewed gift of hope.

PART SEVEN

Maddie Medical Update (10/10/17)

Team Maddie,

Today is a day of strength for the Kramer girls. Lily played her part in keeping the family healthy this winter by getting her flu shot. Mommy reported live from the scene that Lily (aka Lily Bug aka Lily Poo aka Big Lil aka Notorious L.I.L.) didn't even wince. She just smiled up at her Mommy and went on her way. Nothing like a protective pad of pudge to prohibit pain!

Maddie then followed her sister's lead, as the doctors confirmed that Maddie is cleared to begin Round VI tomorrow. This marks the first time Maddie hasn't been delayed to start a round on account of blood counts. Her recovery from Round V, and strength throughout, is nothing short of amazing.

Round VI brings five consecutive days of outpatient chemo (the first few of which will largely be all-day infusions). Here's to a fast and fun five days. To a Round VI that is anywhere comparable to Round V. And to Lily's incomparable cheeks.

First Row (10/15/17)

C hildhood and milestones are inseparable. The list of firsts alone is an endless wonder. First smile. First bath. First coo. First words. First steps.

Pammy and I never missed a moment to memorialize a milestone. Life A.C. is no different in that respect. They might not write about this one in the baby books, but that's not stopping us from marking the occasion. When the chemo process started, the medical team handed us a written protocol that outlines every treatment round with letters symbolizing the specific treatment for each week. As each treatment comes to a close, Pammy checks off the completed letter, and we do a little celebratory handshake. Gimmicky? Perhaps. But no less inspirational with each touch of our hands. And remember, never miss a moment to memorialize a milestone.

Overall, the mile-long treatment portion of the protocol maps out visually into three rows. Today marks the end of the first row of treatments. In the 16 weeks comprising the first row (which has been more like 20-plus calendar weeks), we have crossed off 44 letters. That's right, 44 chemo-related treatments. We also never miss a chance for a symbolic reference to #44 himself, Anthony Rizzo. Did I mention we finished off Round VI in Room 44? Although 2 rows, 36 weeks, and 11 rounds of chemo remain, the first row was voluminous in every which way. Voluminous in medications. Voluminous in hospital stays. Voluminous in smiles. Voluminous in tears. Voluminous in hope. Voluminous in fears.

But as we gripped our first row seat through the volume of the first row, Maddie never ceased to amaze. With one row down, the volume of inpatient therapies also starts to dial down. And Maddie continues to dial up her energy. It's been another outstanding week in Maddie Kramer's Neighborhood. She's almost spoiling us at this point. Maddie has been in such phenomenal spirits, we sometimes can't help even forgetting what brings us to Lurie's Place in the first place.

Unfortunately, the humbling reminders are never too far away. Starting next week, we journey toward the second row and re-enter the window where Maddie's counts drop, and she attempts to fight off the dreaded F'n Ns stay.

Whatever the second row holds, we'll hold on to our first row seats. Because our prized fighter deserves every ounce of loving support. We didn't ask for these tickets. But since they're apparently nonrefundable (believe me, I've begged whatever divinity holds the StubHub password for this hopefully forgiving account), we'll do our best to keep the music, dancing, smiles, and spirits going strong.

And don't think we've taken our eye off the milestone ball in the meantime. 2 days ago, Lily turned a whopping 8 months old. Happy Birthday, Lily Bug! Never miss a moment to memorialize a milestone.

Maddie Medical Update (10/21/17)

Team Maddie,

11 days have officially passed since Round VI began. Only once before has Maddie made it this far out without an F'n Ns stay (and that was last round, when Maddie avoided Lurie's Place altogether).

Maddie hasn't missed a beat this round. She had a brief platelets transfusion today but has been all laughs and smiles. We're not sure if Maddie has a repeat miracle performance in her, but she's off to a promising start. Here's to a happy, healthy, home-based weekend!

Maddie Medical Update (10/24/17)

Team Maddie,

Autumn clouds may now fill the skies, but Maddie remains all sunshine. This girl is on fire. Maddie's recovery from Round VI officially broke her previous record. After just 8 consecutive evenings of baby pokes, Maddie's ANC returned to levels sufficient to go back to our ordinary, peaceful bedtime routine. Assuming no delays, that leaves her a full week of fun to gear up for the next round. In other news, rumor has it that Jim Harbaugh has Maddie next in line on the QB depth chart. The Wolverines are in need of a hero who can stay cool under pressure. Maddie seemed like the logical choice.

The Waiting (10/31/17)

Tom Petty had some choice words to say about *The Waiting*. While I'm guessing he didn't have our type of situation in mind when composing his famous chorus, he was certainly onto something.

The A.C. memory that no amount of waiting will suppress takes me back to the Neurosurgery Waiting Room. On April 21st. I say the Waiting Room, but most of my time was not spent in the Waiting Room. I instead paced around the 19th floor hallways for 6 hours straight. My head still reeling from Maddie's MRI results. My brain still swallowed by the image of an intubated Maddie being wheeled off to surgery. My body and mind reduced to near nothingness. Holding on to whatever strength I had left in the name of hope. And in the name of Maddie.

During The Waiting, all I knew was the torment of not knowing. Not knowing how Maddie was doing. Not knowing what precisely the doctors would find. Not knowing how Maddie would emerge. Not knowing if Maddie would emerge. I can close my eyes and still feel my mouth mustering the strength just to mutter, "Come on, Maddie. Come on, kiddo." Trying to will myself with words through The Waiting.

With all due respect to Tom Petty, to say that The Waiting was the hardest part would be a gross understatement. The Waiting was suffocating. The Waiting was heart-piercing. The Waiting was life-crushing. Although in fairness, I guess Tom only had so many words to work with for purposes of creating a catchy chorus.

Just like Tom's catchy chorus, however, we can't quite get The Waiting out of our minds. Every 9 to 11 weeks or so, the Lurie DJs turn up the volume. They play this figurative chorus line on repeat, as we make our way back to the original surgical floor for a follow-up MRI. We are forced to again dip our toes into The Waiting pool. And no matter how much stronger we now are, we can't help but feel the water rise each time.

Yesterday was our next test to stay afloat. Maddie's next scheduled MRI. Our next scheduled day of waiting and making sure the tumor has not come back. On the floor where the first frightening words of Maddie's now inspirational song of life were written. The floor where standing went to collapsing. Where smiles turned to tears. Where light became dark. Where B.C. became A.C.

The feeling of The Waiting in the A.C. World is an odd psychological mix of past and present. We run into Ellen, one of the friendliest nurses who so gracefully navigated us through Maddie's April MRI. We talk like old friends while ignoring the underlying horror that links us. Reliving mental snapshots of our nightmare, we watch as the staff takes Maddie away from us and into the MRI room. The only time – other than April 21st – when physical separation unlinks us from Maddie. And then we wait. Again. Only this time we wait knowing exactly what we're waiting for. Good news or bad news. Thumbs up or thumbs down. It's a wait that, while shorter and more binary than the original Waiting, is equally excruciating.

As we endure this Waiting with more experience than the first go-around, we see others around us on their maiden voyage. I overhear a doctor approach two nervous parents. "Good news, no tumor," he says, as they breathe a sigh of relief. The sigh of relief that Pammy and I so desperately hoped was waiting for us on April 21st. We see other parents clearly not as lucky. As quieter doctors' words yield only tears of pain. The collective waiting in the pediatric surgery waiting room is like a purgatory of the most sacred of all emotions – love and fear for our children. And yet there is nothing more for us to do than wait to hear our name called.

On some level, Maddie has her own awareness of The Waiting. Or at least waiting for her day at Lurie's Place that feels a bit different from the others. When she woke up yesterday morning at 4:50 a.m. on her own accord (yes, 4:50 a.m.), she was already on high alert.

"Daddy, are they going to have the good bubbles for my walk today?" (We always ask the child life specialist, Becca, to blow bubbles for her while she walks to her MRI.)

"Daddy, are you and Mommy going to come with me?"

These nervous questions did not last long though. In typical Maddie fashion, she changed the tune of our group song before we left for Lurie's Place. Maddie's questions quickly turned to clapping. She went from inquiring to singing. And despite Maddie being awake at such an ungodly hour, I couldn't help but join in the fun. I chose to lie waiting, to immerse in The Waiting, and soak in her endless flow of Maddie chatter. I listened to her jokes. I accepted her LEGO invitation. I smiled back and forth in the nightlighted background. I waded in our collective waiting as the clock ticked closer to departure.

The change of tune doesn't stop there. Come 5:30 a.m., Maddie then asks a familiar question with an unfamiliar answer. "Daddy, can we watch *Daniel Tiger*?" TV shows at 5:30 a.m.? A.C. Answer – absolutely! And wouldn't you know, what was the topic in this episode?

Waiting.

Yes, Waiting. I could hardly believe it myself, as I was already dreading The Waiting that awaited us. But our inspirational tiger, Daniel, indeed philosophized about how to deal with The Waiting. OK, so maybe the context was a bit different (an anxious toddler tiger waiting for the food to arrive at a restaurant may *not* be the perfect analogy). But per usual, Daniel's suggestion couldn't have been better. And even more catchy than Mr. Petty.

When you wait, you can play, sing, or imagine anything.

Oh, Daniel. You wise little tiger. Daniel's sing-songy message is spot on. We don't need to just wait passively. We can take that waiting and make it play time, song time, or imagination time. We can try and live through The Waiting and not just wait through The Waiting. Leave it to Daniel and Maddie to give us direction on this next installment of The Waiting.

And so went the rest of our morning of "waiting." Maddie chatted her way through the drive down Lake Shore to Lurie's Place. Maddie colored her way through the waiting room. Maddie *Goldie & Bear'd* her way through the pre-scan hospital room time. Maddie bubbled her way through the MRI walk. While we adults may have a tendency to just wait and anxiously ruminate on what is ahead, Maddie doesn't stop playing. She doesn't stop singing. She doesn't stop imagining. Daniel would be proud of our little tiger.

At least for today, I have a different take on The Waiting. I was blessed to wait yesterday. I will be blessed to wait 9 to 11 weeks from now. I would be blessed to wait forever. After all, waiting means there is someone to wait for. Because there's only one thing that I cannot wait for...

To see that beautiful smile that comes after The Waiting.

With that in mind, we're changing up the theme song for this week. Forget *The Waiting*. I've decided that Mumford & Sons has a far better take on waiting. Go online and start playing Mumford & Sons' *I Will Wait*. And listen away as you read the P.S. note below.

P.S. With the banjo now blasting in the background, there's no waiting needed for the results to Maddie's MRI. The scan came back clean today. Maddie was thus cleared to begin the Second Row of treatments. The first of eight rounds in this Second Row. Hey, you've got to break it down to avoid breaking down. Watch out, Round 2.1. Maddie is ready and waiting. And we will wait for you, sweet girl.

The Audience (11/7/17)

Last Saturday night, Pammy and I hopped in the car with Maddie for a special trip. The route was all too familiar. We headed east on Addison. We passed Wrigley Field. We started driving south on Lake Shore Drive. We waved hi to Maddie's preschool. We approached the exit for Lurie's Place. And then, it happened. Something new. Something exciting. Something remarkable.

We kept going.

Saturday marked the first time in 7 months that we kept going. The first time in 7 months that we drove south on Lake Shore at any point after 12:00 p.m. when we weren't headed straight to Lurie's Place. How I wanted to step on the gas, roll down the windows, and just blare any song by a lead singer who was not a cartoon character. But knowing that Lurie's Place was not our final landing spot this evening was enough of a reward for me. Mommy, Maddie, and Daddy had bigger fish to fry. Or shall I say, Pigs.

Our destination? Peppa Pig. Live at The Chicago Theatre. Right up there with Springsteen on Broadway. With our hospital masks in tow, we anxiously decided to brave the snotty surroundings for this once-in-a-lifetime opportunity. An opportunity courtesy of a very special not-for-profit, Bear Necessities, which gifted Maddie this "Bear Hug." And what a hug it was.

After five straight days of Pammy having to play doctor, nurse, and negotiator (and successfully convincing Maddie to digest chemo orally for the first of two times in this protocol), we couldn't wait to jump in Peppa's proverbial muddy puddles.

When we entered the theater, Maddie had no idea what was to come. Her nerves were palpable. Was it anticipation? Excitement? Curiosity? As the curtains rose to the narrator's squealing voice, the answer could not have been more apparent.

It was raw terror! Maddie gripped me with her own horrified Bear Hug, as she averted her eyes and burrowed into my armpit cave.

Pammy and I couldn't help but smile. Multiple surgeries, body-ravaging chemo, nightly subcutaneous shots, and endless hospital stays. Apparently, that's all child's play. Seeing one of her favorite characters come to life on a downtown theater stage? Sound the swine alarms!

As much as I would've silently taken solace in Maddie sweating something small for a change, it didn't take her long to warm up. In no time she was clapping and singing along with Peppa, George, Mummy and Daddy Pig, and the ever-underrated Mr. Potato.

What a miraculous moment. For months, whether she knows it or not, Maddie has been at the center of her own stage. We've had the first row seat to a show that in every which way revolved around Maddie's medical care. But on Saturday night, for nearly ninety minutes of nonstop and noisy nonsense, Maddie was able to secure a different seat. A seat as just an ordinary member of an audience. An audience full of other children brought together by nothing more than a pink pig and her family and friends.

Needless to say, we all felt the warm, fuzzy fur of this charitable "Bear Hug." And so as we headed home on Lake

Shore Drive at 7:00 p.m., we passed Lurie's Place without pausing. We didn't talk about The Playroom. We didn't chat about our favorite nurses. We didn't hype up our next stay at Lurie's Place. We didn't revisit The Narrative. We just reminisced about our brief yet beautiful time in the audience. At someone else's show. Well worthy of an encore.

The Power of One (11/11/17)

This week, Pammy powered up her work laptop. A laptop that was first closed when Pammy transitioned to maternity leave in February 2017. A laptop that remained shuttered when maternity leave spilled into personal leave in April 2017.

In the wake of Maddie's surgery, there were a lot of puzzle pieces we had to put together. As two working parents, we knew sacrifices were necessary. Someone had to be home with Maddie. For both Maddie's emotional and physical survival, just continuing to waltz both of us off to work wouldn't be workable. In piecing that puzzle together, Pammy and I also knew that she was going to be the One. That Pammy would be the corner pieces to Maddie's cancer puzzle.

The only catch? Maddie was covered on Pammy's health insurance (of course, why not add that sour ingredient to the mental mix that was life A.C.). For better or worse, we tested out a newly-acquired A.C. trait for two otherwise Type A parents – we made a decision based on the now not the unknown. We agreed to focus on what Maddie needed right then. Right there. Even if that meant deferring the looming cloud of insurance until Pammy's leave expired on November 8th (a date that felt like an eternity from our April 21st decision). And what Maddie needed right then and there was a stable force at home. She needed her Mommy.

Since April 21st, there are no words to describe, nor can any of us truly appreciate, what Pammy's experience has been like. Day in and day out, she has been right in the trenches with Maddie. Every smile. Every tear. Every dance. Every fear. Every doctor visit. Every painful minute. Every dessert. Every hurt.

While the rest of the familial side of Team Maddie at least has pockets of reprieve and moments to unplug – whether that be going to work, spending time alone with friends, etc. – Pammy hasn't been afforded that luxury. There are no breaks. No reprieves. No moments to unplug. Pammy has been as closely connected to Maddie as the central line running through the veins linking to Maddie's heart. They are One.

Yet in all that time, with all that pressure, not once have I seen a crack in the foundation. A waver of strength. A blockage in the connection. Pammy has been plugged into Maddie and keeping her fully charged without error. Both of them powering forward with perpetual positivity.

You often hear people describe their significant others as a rock. Let's be clear. Pammy is not just a rock. She is a f*cking boulder encased in bulletproof tactical gear. A woman of unimaginable force who went from enjoying the delicate balance of working mom to the unwavering and gut-wrenching world of warrior mom.

This week represents a miraculous moment for our fearless, familial leader. The week Pammy reincorporates another weapon into her war chest. The week she rediscovers the ability to plug into something other than Maddie. The week she reconnects to a story beyond The Narrative. The week she reboots her laptop.

The underlying power in that laptop, and all the forces that went into re-charging its batteries, are equally impressive. Since 2010, Pammy has been employed by

PepsiCo. Specifically, she's spent time in various finance roles for their Quaker Oats and Tropicana divisions (public service announcement, PepsiCo is *not just a soda company*).

A few years ago, PepsiCo promoted "The Power of One." On Wall Street, this motto was used to tout the triumph of maintaining various, diverse lines of business. But from my spousal sightline, this team-oriented tagline also exhibited the collaborative and united nature of the PepsiCo workforce. Since Pammy started working at PepsiCo, I never ceased to be amazed at the level of camaraderie among colleagues, whether bosses, counterparts, or underlings. They were a team. They were One.

And that Oneness could not have been on fuller display during Pammy's personal leave. Just because her laptop powered down did not mean that her PepsiCo connection sputtered. Pammy's PepsiCo family continued their ongoing support, as Pammy navigated Maddie from the stormy seas of April 21st into the steady ship that has sailed into this Second Row of treatment. Through e-mails, text messages, home visits, and hospital visits, their Oneness was ever-present.

As Pammy's personal leave approached its November 8th expiration, however, the water levels began to rise again on the Kramer ship. Where do we turn for insurance for Maddie? More importantly, what does Pammy's professional future hold? We should've known better than to drown in these questions. Because true teams don't fail their teammates in trying times. In a world where the idea of a big corporation has become a synonym for something sinister, PepsiCo reminded all of us of the love and support incorporated by a true corporation. They did so with a most unexpected and amazing gesture, which only the sweetness of a can of Pepsi could match.

In the weeks leading up to November 8th, the PepsiCo leadership offered Pammy a part-time role. A role that gives her the power to work from home. I can't underestimate the power packed into this position. For Pammy, this represents more than just the power to power up a laptop in a more personal setting. It's the power to keep Maddie protectively insured. The power to continue to be Maddie's primary protector while also piecing back together her professional prowess. The power to plug into something other than the cancer outlet. The power to support her PepsiCo peers who propped her up during this perilous period.

The Power of One.

Maddie Medical Update (11/13/17)

Team Maddie,

Round 2.1 (Round 1 of 8 in the Second Row) has officially come to a close, as Maddie successfully concluded her post-2.1 baby poke routine without an F'n Ns stay. For those keeping score at home, that's three consecutive rounds without a chemo-induced hospital stay. The drought is so long that Maddie is at the point where she's disappointed when she hears we're not going to Lurie's Place. You have to wonder if The Narrative was *too successful* when you hear Maddie say excitedly, "I just can't wait for my next sleepover!"

The good news doesn't stop there. Without question, Maddie is in the best spirits since her chemotherapy began. The only thing matching her energy is her appetite. So much so that the nutrition team is in the process of attempting to wean her off TPN (the liquid nutrition infused through her central line every night) over the course of the next couple weeks.

The icing on this post-chemo cake? The gap between the start of Round 2.1 and Round 2.2 is 4 weeks, the longest gap in the protocol. The only time that happens again is in between Rounds 2.2 and 2.3 before returning to tri-weekly treatments. Needless to say, we hopefully have a happy, healthy, and hungry conclusion to 2017 (can a Daddy get a "poo poo poo"?)!

Thank you all for your unending support. Team Maddie is as strong as ever.

A Perfect Moment (An Ode to Dr. Alden) (11/16/17)

"She looks perfect."

Those three words gracefully flowed from the mouth of Maddie's Super Doctor, Dr. Alden, at her routine surgical follow-up at 8:30 a.m. this morning.

Doctors have uttered a lot of words to us over the course of the past 7 months. But let's just say that "she looks perfect" hasn't received much air time.

The source of these three words was even more remarkable. The surgeon who met Maddie at her most imperfect time. The surgeon who, in the early hours of April 21st, warned us of the grave risks associated with Maddie's emergency surgery. The surgeon who, with incredible precision, removed a tumor covering 4 levels of Maddie's spine. The surgeon who carried Maddie from paralysis to miraculous. The surgeon who saved Maddie's life. The surgeon who blessed our lives.

Although we met Dr. Alden in the darkest depths of our nightmare, our surgical savior kept our dreams alive. And so every follow-up visit comes with an unfathomable feeling of awe. Imagine having the opportunity to stand face-to-face with the person who literally saved your child's life. Imagine watching this gentle giant – standing easily above 6'2" with a build more like a football player than a pediatric surgeon

— kindly converse with his 36-inch patient about everything from her pink shoes to her favorite Peppa character. Imagine our elder hero then witness his toddler sidekick jump up and down fancifully on the same feet we feared wouldn't flow together again.

"Imagine" is in many ways a perfect word. Because even sitting in the patient room live we can't help but feel like maybe we are still dreaming. Only the nightmare is in our rearview mirror. And what's the view like today? Well, she looks perfect.

Thank you, Dr. Alden. I'm still not convinced you're real. But I have no doubt that you made our dreams a reality.

Unchained Melody (11/22/17)

Picture this.

Someone plucks you from your ordinary life without warning. You're transported to the middle of a remote part of the Pacific Ocean. You're dropped into the water. The sky is dark. The waves are choppy. You're told there *may* be a life raft some 20 miles away. But you won't know for sure until you get there. So you start swimming. With all your might. Only tied to your legs is a chain. And on that chain, each and every day, five pounds of weight are added. Dragging you further and further under.

Welcome to the first 60 days of life A.C. I should say days 14-60. Because lord knows no metaphor in the world will adequately capture the first 14 days.

I'll never forget the night when what felt like the final five-pound weight was added. The weight that almost brought us under. In retrospect, it almost sounds silly. A comparatively innocuous event. Nowhere near the intensity of the other challenges or trauma we had faced previously. But let's face it, we were somewhere around Day 30 of treading water in the A.C. World. The waves were covering our mouths but barely leaving a centimeter for our nostrils to take those fighting breaths. Any added weight, no matter how small, risked drowning.

The form of this seemingly final five-pound weight? A five-pound black bag called TPN – Total Parenteral Nutrition. A black bag that we were required to connect to Maddie's central line nightly via a two-foot small plastic tube charged with delivering nutrition to Maddie over a 12-hour period. Unable to manage sufficient food or water intake on her own, Maddie relied on this literal and figurative ball and chain for strength and sustenance. And for more than 150 days now, the ball and chain has provided just that.

The need for TPN wasn't on our radar. Like all things A.C., the medical team delivered challenging news slowly. Day by day adding their five-pound weights, so as not to break our spirits on our swim for life. So when the home health nurse arrived that evening, Pammy and I really didn't know what to expect. But there she stood. A sweet, little gray-haired lady. She could've been a stand-in for one of the Golden Girls. Not exactly the Grim Reaper type who I would expect to deliver a ball and chain. I almost felt badly that she had to be the messenger. She gently walked us through the instructions for setting up the TPN. She arrived around 5:30 p.m. She finished somewhere around 8:00 p.m. We spent 2.5 painstaking hours of instruction and setup together. 2.5 hours that we didn't have room to accommodate, as our days were already replete with more medications and burdensome routines than we could ever fathom. And yet as the nurse connected Maddie to this seemingly final five-pound weight, what did Pammy and I do?

We laughed.

Uncontrollable, tear-inducing laughter. Battered. Exhausted. Water levels rising. Desperately trying to continue our way to the life raft in the distance. And yet our internal survival sensors said to laugh.

Maybe it was the exhaustion. Maybe the exasperation. Maybe we were just going a little stir crazy. In any case, we knew we were in over our heads. The absurdity of life A.C. hit us harder than the crashing waves. And with each laugh we could feel the weights releasing. We could feel ourselves swimming back to the top of the ocean. Resuming our journey.

In the 150-plus days since the ball and chain first arrived, we've been making the most of the TPN Experience. And wouldn't you know, we got pretty good at it. Pammy is now probably 90% finished with her self-taught oncology home health degree, as she learned to whip up the TPN concoction in under 30 minutes. All things told, TPN still probably added around two hours of tasks to each day (including a 3:00 a.m. alarm to change Maddie's diaper to ensure the extra hydration didn't flood her bed). But we made due and just kept swimming.

Despite our ability to adapt, it was still challenging to watch the ball and chain restrain Maddie. Every morning, the ball and chain is there. I carry Maddie downstairs. She is on one shoulder, and the ball and chain are on the other. For the hour or so each morning that the TPN continues to flow, an adult has to play guard to the prisoner of this nutrition war. Hovering close as Maddie dances, walks, and plays within the radius of her two-foot chain. Freedom arrives somewhere between 7:30 and 8:30 a.m. every day when Warden Mommy breaks the chain.

When evening arrives, Maddie settles into The Nook. But not before being re-chained to the ball. Although it doesn't stop us from our nightly concert, there is still something awkward about the walk to the Princess Bed. Maddie in one arm. The ball and chain balancing in the other. Needing to lay down the ball and chain before laying down Maddie. Careful to avoid stepping on the chain during the *And We Bid You Goodnight* portion of the slow dance to her bed. I make due. But the ball and chain are always there.

Always weighing us down a bit, if only with just five pounds worth of resistance.

Not surprisingly, Maddie remains unfazed by the chains. She has been able to shuckle while shackled. Have a ball with the ball. Every morning, as the TPN freedom alarm rings between 7:30 and 8:30 a.m., Maddie excitedly shouts, "Mommy, it's done!" Not so much because she needs relief as that she'll take any opportunity to celebrate.

Well tonight, Maddie, we join in your celebration. Because tomorrow morning, for the first time in more than 150 days, you won't be the one shouting, "It's Done!" Instead, it'll be Mommy and Daddy shouting from the Wrigleyville Rooftops, *"She's Done!"* Because more than 150 days later, Maddie is now eating and drinking sufficiently to cut the TPN ball and chain. To dance unchained. To sing unchained. To Nook unchained. To live unchained.

Now picture this:

You can slowly see your ordinary life returning. With your chains removed, you're now swimming at full speed. You even see the shoreline albeit far in the distance. The sky is now bright and beautiful. The waves have smoothed out. You have no doubt as to whether there is a life raft waiting for you. Instead, you realize your life raft has been there all along. All three feet (and a half an inch) and 30 pounds of her. And as the sun goes down, without the weight of the ball and chain, you squeeze that life raft tighter than you have in more than 150 days. Knowing that you'll continue to swim together. Stronger and faster than ever.

Feeling Full (11/23/17)

I feel full. Literally. I am absolutely stuffed. Not that I should be surprised. For the first time ever, two titans of Turkey Day – Grandma Sue and Gaga – combined culinary forces for an epic Thanksgiving feast. It was like a food-based greatest hits record from both sides of our family album. Everything from meatballs to spinach balls. Mashed potatoes to sweet potatoes. French roast to roasted turkey. Quite a meal and quite a moment for Maddie's matriarchal mentors.

But let's face it. On this Thanksgiving Day, my fullness extends well beyond my bloated belly. I am emotionally and spiritually full. Busting at my psychological seams. With Maddie by all accounts approaching full strength, we cannot help but feel equally full of pride, gratitude, and joy.

We took 30 minutes out of our holiday celebration today to enjoy our usual walk to the local elementary school tot lot. But there was something extraordinary about today's walk despite the ordinary route. Maddie was walking with renewed strength. No tripping. No loss of balance. She just pounded the pavement with her pink Peppa shoes. She conquered the miniature "climbing wall" without anything but a spotter. She scaled the swirly slide backward, basically bear walking from the bottom of the slide up. Her seven months of post-surgical success on full display. With the sun shining down on us during this unseasonably warm

Thanksgiving Day, Pammy and I felt like someone was basting us with blessings. Allowing us to watch Maddie in all of her physically recovered glory on the ultimate day of thanks.

Our attitude of gratitude does not stop there. While we all count our blessings to some degree on Thanksgiving, what hit me especially hard this year was the sheer volume of people for whom I felt thankful. For the past 48 hours, I've been cycling through the full mental Rolodex of those who have helped us stay fully afloat in this year of survival. People who are responsible for saving Maddie's life. People who are responsible for enriching Maddie's life. People who have prayed. People who have stayed. People who have given. People who have driven. People who have gifted. People who have lifted. People who lended an ear. People who shared a tear. People who believed. People who helped us achieve. People who have joined in a song. People who have read along.

Ultimately, the bounds of our gratitude run as deep as Team Maddie's full roster. You all have no idea how much your collective love has filled our lives. We are fully aware. And fully grateful.

On thankful reflection, when A.C. life began, one of the many choices Pammy and I had was how to cope and with whom to cope. I don't think either of us typically requested assistance with, let alone invited others into, our private lives. But there was nothing typical about April 21st and after. So as tempting as it was to shut down, to restrict access, and to limit detail, we made the literal and figurative decision to become an open book. And the meaning of our family's story is so much fuller as a result. Thanks to you, we are not – and have never been – alone in the A.C. World. We truly are Team Maddie. And while we all know there is no "I" in team, there is most certainly an "I" in Maddie. An "I" that she deserves fully. Because there is no doubt that Maddie's singular strength, brightness, and resilience serve as the inspirational force that continues to keep all of our spirits full.

Full of love. Full of gratitude. Full of Maddie-tude. Feeling full never felt so good.

Maddie Medical Update (11/28/17)

Team Maddie,

Maddie was cleared to begin Round 2.2 today (Round 2 of 8 in this Second Row of treatments). Maddie's presence on the pre-fight scale was astounding. One week removed from the ball and chain, Maddie is maintaining a weight of 29.5 pounds (the 50th percentile)! She also continued to defy odds of Kramer Gravity, as her height increased to 36.8 inches. No word yet on her reach or vertical.

Round 2.2 is a repeat of Round 2.1. It consists of 5 consecutive days of Oral Chemo. While we hope the side effects prove to be manageable again, the administration is beyond taxing on Pammy and Maddie. But we have our plan of attack. Oral Chemo is no match for the ChiP Strategy:

Chocolate chips
iPad
Prize

The ChiP Strategy proved unbeatable in Round 2.1. We're not about to ruin a good thing. Here's to a similar success story for 2.2. Thank you for all of your support!

Miracles and Lights (12/11/17)

M iracles and Lights. At its core, that's what the holiday season is about. Depending on your particular religious persuasion, it's just a matter of which Miracles and which Lights. Our family's celebration begins tomorrow with the first night of Hanukkah. As Adam Sandler has taught us, Hanukkah is the "Festival of Lights." But believe it or not, there's more to Hanukkah than David Lee Roth and Hall of Famer, Rod Carew.

My CliffsNotes version of this B.C. (the *other* B.C.) story? After rebelling against a tyrannical regime, a group of biblical heroes reclaimed their holy temple. In order to sanctify their reclamation, they were required to light a *menorah* for eight days. There was one problem. They only had one little cruse of oil. An amount presumed sufficient to burn for just one day as opposed to the requisite eight. Enter the Miracle that joined the Light. This teeny bit of oil ended up lasting all eight days. Hence, the eight days of Hanukkah. A celebration of Miracles and Lights.

These two words bring a unique sense of joy this year. Our year of Miracles. Our year of Lights. And to think both have come in the form of our three-year-old hero. The girl whose own light began to dim on April 21st. The girl who embodied Miracle in her surgical recovery that followed. The girl who shines Light day in and day out. The girl whose personification of Miracles and Lights has now reached its eighth straight month of A.C. wonder, as we approach our eight-day celebration of Miracles and Lights.

For me and Pammy, however, the celebration of Miracles and Lights began much earlier than life A.C. When Maddie was born, we cherished our firsthand experience with the miracle of life and the resulting light. In doing so, that June 26th afternoon, Pammy and I also announced Maddie's Hebrew name. For many Jewish couples, the idea of bestowing a Hebrew name is a meaningful method to memorialize a beloved family member. In Maddie's case, the "M" from both her English and Hebrew name was a tribute to Pammy's grandmother, Mary. A miraculous maternal figure in her own right (and a maven of mondel bread to boot). But apparently there may have been some other symbolic forces at work behind Maddie's name as well.

Maddie's Hebrew name? *Mira.*
Three letters short of the word she's delivered to us all.

The meaning of Maddie's Hebrew name? *Light.*
Miracles and Lights.

Quite a combination that has illuminated inspiration since June 26, 2014. Miraculously joined by our chubby-cheeked cherub on February 13, 2017. Maddie's partner in exuberance, Lily, whose Hebrew name – Leora – means none other than: "I have light." Maddie and Lily. Miracles and Lights. Ms and Ls.

Today marks another victory for Miracles and Lights. The official conclusion of Round 2.2. The end of Maddie's eight crazy nights of baby pokes. Maddie's fourth consecutive round without an F'n Ns stay. Maddie's 82nd consecutive night sleeping in her own Princess Bed instead of a Lurie's Place hospital bed. And Maddie's seemingly infinite night of bringing light where there would otherwise be darkness.

And so as we light the *menorah* with our little M and little L, we will give thanks for the many Miracles and Lights that have graced our year. And to all of Team Maddie this holiday season: regardless of which Miracles you will be cherishing, and which Lights you will be celebrating, here's to many more Miracles. And to endless Lights.

PART EIGHT

Maddie Medical Update (12/18/17)

Team Maddie,

Maddie's miraculous journey took an unexpected and frightening turn this weekend. After Maddie randomly experienced head pain and vomiting on Saturday afternoon, we headed to the Lurie's Place Emergency Room. Upon review of Maddie's MRI, the doctors found a concerning, five-millimeter spot near Maddie's tumor site. We do not have definitive answers or conclusions at this time. The medical team is regrouping as we speak, and we expect to hear more on next steps later in the week. We understand they will be considering various treatment options moving forward. While there is no sugar coating the implications of these results, Maddie's wonderful oncologist, Dr. Jason, confirmed we are not necessarily at the end of the treatment road pending additional testing.

Not surprising to any of us, Maddie has been a rock star all weekend. When she emerged from her preliminary, "quick" MRI, Maddie was thrilled to find out that she was finally getting to sleep over again at Lurie's Place. She had the nurses all in stitches with her excitement. The only toddler in the world who can't wait to sleep over at the hospital. With good reason – Maddie returned to her favorite playroom for the first time in nearly three months, received a surprise visit from Pammy's dear friend, Neha (who, upon arrival, was appointed by Maddie to play the role of Galleria from *Creative Galaxy*), and experienced a special YouTube viewing of *Miffy the Movie*, an epic bedtime classic. To Maddie's indifference, we were then released to come home on Sunday evening as the doctors reconvened. After asking for "just one more song" for four consecutive bedtime tunes, Maddie finally went to sleep peacefully for a well-deserved rest.

At this point, while Maddie's MRI may have changed, our approach and goals have not. We will continue to love. We will continue to hope. We will continue to dance. We will continue to sing. We will continue to pray for Miracles and Lights. And we will continue, with every ounce of our beings, to keep Maddie as Maddie.

Thank you for all of your prayers and support.

You Are My Sunshine (12/18/17)

"Daddy, I can't see the sun anymore."

Maddie whispered this observation while laying on my shoulder and looking out her Lurie's Place window on Sunday morning. Only she wasn't referring to the actual sun. Instead, she was referring to the office building that faces her Lurie's Place room window. This particular office building faces all Lurie's Place rooms with a northern view. We've stayed in these rooms a few times, and they clearly left their mark on Maddie.

Where does the sun come into this? The employees of the office building collaborated to display window-sized construction paper pictures to face Lurie's Place. It was their creative way to bring joy to the little patients. During the summer, you could find pictures of things like ice cream, a ladybug, and Maddie's beloved sun. But as the employees converted to their winter-themed pictures, the sun disappeared from our Lurie's Place view.

So when Maddie whispered those words on my shoulders, I knew immediately she wasn't referring to the real sun. But my heart sank nonetheless. Because for the first time in months, as the construction paper sun disappeared out of sight, the brightness from Lurie's Place was also sucked back into the darkness. At the moment Maddie noticed the missing sun, we were nearly two hours into our painful, seven-hour wait for final MRI results. Praying the sun would return from behind the clouds in the form of positive MRI news, but knowing that the long wait for feedback was likely an ominous preview.

The events leading up to this moment were equally as ominous. On Saturday afternoon, at around 12:30 p.m., Maddie and I were just playing in our playroom at home. Out of nowhere, Maddie pointed randomly to the back of her head.

"Daddy, it hurts," she said.

My body immediately froze. My heart went into my throat. It was a complete flashback to April 2017. When B.C. became A.C. I tried to ignore the flood of fears. I tried to re-focus on playing with Maddie.

Ten minutes later, "Daddy, it still hurts."

Pammy and I exchange anxious glances. We agree that I need to call Lurie's Place. I pick up the phone and call the emergency room. I explain the situation to the oncologist on-call. She says that for the time being we can continue to monitor Maddie's symptoms from home. Although the location is concerning, we do not need to come to the emergency room unless Maddie presents other symptoms such as vomiting or dizziness.

Five minutes later, Maddie vomits intensely. Darkness chokes my throat. All of our hopes and all of our progress over the last few months are being spewed into our master bathroom toilet. Pammy calmly gathers our things. We wrap Maddie in a blanket, and I carry her on my shoulder as we walk to our garage. I pull my keys from my pocket. I press unlock. There's no sound. Our car is dead. The same car we bought in April 2014, just weeks before Maddie was born.

No time to dwell on symbolism. Fortunately, my dad and sister are at our house. We rush back inside and ask for the keys to my dad's car. Only problem? He has no car seat. No matter. I hop in the back seat holding a frail and exhausted Maddie. Pammy takes the wheel. We head east on Addison Street toward Lake Shore Drive. We barely say a word to one another. Our faces express our few and fearful thoughts.

Suddenly, Pammy screams, "Look, it's Dr. Jason!"

Maddie's oncologist happens to be walking his dog down Addison just as we are making our way to the hospital. Of the millions of people living in Chicago, we run into Maddie's oncologist in the middle of this ominous trip of terror. I react instinctively.

"Pull over!" I yell.

I run out of the car, with Maddie still in my arms, without any idea of what I'm hoping to say or accomplish.

"Dr. Jason! Dr. Jason!"

A few screams later, he turns around startled. We have a quick exchange. He prays that it's just a viral infection and promises to check in with the oncologist on-call. Maddie and I hop back in the car. A few words and all-too-many fear-filled thoughts later, we arrive in the Emergency Room. They know we're coming and take us right away. We settle Maddie into her room. Per our usual routine, we shuffle between Nick Jr. and Disney Jr. on the television. Pammy stays in the room to bring normalcy to Maddie and manage the nurses. I guard the door to ensure all medical conversations take place away from Maddie.

No sooner do I step outside than do I see her. The same doctor who was on call the night of April 20th. The same doctor who had the insight to request an MRI for Maddie that evening. The same doctor who saw through the distractions of Maddie's cold symptoms, neck pain, and hand rashes. The same doctor who made the call that ultimately saved Maddie's life that evening. Here she was again. Despite numerous ER visits since April 20th, it's the first time we've seen each other since that night. And once again, this time holding back tears, she calmly relays that we need to order an MRI.

Approximately 24 hours later, we learned the MRI results. One five-millimeter spot at the base of Maddie's tumor site. Five millimeters looming large over 5,000 hours of miraculous medical momentum. Maddie went from paralysis to miraculous. She climbed to the other side of the Mega Treatment Mountain. She cruised to the conclusion of her First Row of chemotherapy. Yet these five little millimeters were now going to enormously alter her entire medical course. And for the first time since April, I was worried that I could no longer see the sun. Just as Maddie's window-facing sun disappeared into the bitter cold of winter.

But on reflection, Maddie and I were both wrong. The only reason we couldn't see the sun had nothing to do with clouds. Or winter. Maddie couldn't see the sun because she was looking into a Lurie's Place window instead of a mirror. And I was dwelling in my mind instead of focusing on Maddie. These five millimeters may have altered Maddie's treatment course, but our little sunshine is still as bright as ever. Despite the dark clouds hovering over us, Maddie's light keeps us going. Maddie hasn't stopped playing since she woke up in her own bed on Monday morning. Her cast of characters eagerly awaited her return. They were rewarded by Maddie breathing life into their little plastic bodies. Creating wondrous, imaginative scenes more suited for a five or six-year-old. And simultaneously breathing life, and providing light, to those of us with the privilege to be by her side.

Keep shining, sweet girl. You are our sunshine.

Maddie Medical Update (12/19/17)

W e were scheduled to return to Lurie's Place today (now Tuesday) at 11:30 a.m. The game plan was to take a sample of fluid both from Maddie's Ommaya Reservoir (essentially, an access point to fluid around her brain) as well as from the fluid around her spinal cord. The doctors would then test those samples for cancer cells to determine the extent of the harm going on inside Maddie's central nervous system beyond the five-millimeter spot.

Unfortunately, Cancer doesn't appear to be sticking to the plan lately. Maddie woke up again with more severe head pain. She was visibly tired despite a full night's sleep. And she vomited a few times before 8:00 a.m. Her morning toys and joys were replaced with morning tears and fears for the first time in months.

Thankfully, her medical team was beyond responsive. After a few early morning e-mail exchanges, they ask us to come in sooner than planned for an evaluation. Pammy and Maddie arrive by 9:00 a.m. The doctors advise that the pain she's experiencing as well as the underlying nausea do not connect logically with the five-millimeter spot on the MRI. She shouldn't be having that much of a reaction to such a small intruder. Something else must be going on. Two cerebrospinal fluid samples (the test results of which are still pending) and one CT scan later, we still do not have any definitive answers.

Per usual, Maddie won't let any of the symptoms or uncertainty keep us down for too long. After waking up from her anesthesia induced slumber, Maddie perks up for the first time all day, looks at the nurse hovering over her, and asks, "Can you get the *good* blood pressure?"

"Which one is that, Maddie?" the nurse replies.

Dr. Maddie responds promptly, "the *manual* blood pressure."

Three years old. Asking for the manual blood pressure. You never cease to amaze us all, Maddie. That amazement for me and Pammy, however, remained clouded in confusion and terror as the night wore on. Dr. Jason confirmed that, in light of Maddie's symptoms, we'll have to stay inpatient again. They're going to start a steroid regimen to help with the pain. He hypothesizes that one of the potential causes of her symptoms could be a barrage of cancer cells occupying the cerebrospinal fluid surrounding her brain (a question which will be answered by the fluid sample tests). It's almost unfathomable that just a few days ago we were riding high on the strength of what felt like the peak of Maddie's recovery, and now we're sinking into a black hole of MRI spots and cancer cells. For tonight, as the fluid sample test results will not be available until tomorrow morning, we are left to another evening of waiting.

Not that Maddie's complaining. She can't wait for her second Lurie's Place sleepover in four days. She's making up for lost time. Cue *Miffy the Movie*. Here's to a peaceful evening with our sweet girl.

Better When We're Dancing (12/19/17)

M addie came out of the womb dancing. Well, not literally. But after arriving two weeks beyond Pammy's due date, we all were eager to get moving with our 6 pound and 11 ounce miracle. And so dance we did. Constantly. Other than changing diapers and cleaning bottles, I have very few lasting memories from Maddie's infancy beyond holding her sweet, swaddled self in my arms while my legs bounced to the beat of song after song after song. The Daddy/Maddie dance is probably my only form of post-fatherhood exercise, and it represents one of the more special exhibitions of our unbreakable bond.

Maddie hasn't stopped dancing since. Anyone who has visited Maddie in the past few months knows that no day is complete without a Maddie Dance Party. And thankfully, we've come a long way since the days of the Disney-only playlist. Your typical Maddie Dance Party will also now include at least some of the following: Coldplay (*Something Just Like This*); The Beatles (*Ob-La-Di, Ob-La-Da*); Taylor Swift (*Shake It Off*); Justin Timberlake (*Can't Stop the Feeling!*); and, without fail, Meghan Trainor (*Better When I'm Dancin'*).

The latter has been somewhat of a motivational anthem during life A.C. As you can imagine, even when Maddie has been riding high, the roller coaster of emotions has been ever-present. All of those feelings funnel into a full smile when you have the pleasure of blasting *Better When I'm*

Dancin' with our three-year-old diva shaking her tush to each toe-tapping tune. Maddie's dancing is the essence of her beautiful and bright spirit. Tumor be damned, Maddie has been dancing while cancering for 8 months now. For me, there is no more inspirational sight in this world.

And so in these past 48 hours, when left with nothing but my wandering mind, I did what Maddie would do:

I danced.

As the what-if, what-once-was, and the what-could-be infiltrated my mind, I fought back by standing on my tired and tearful feet, and by dancing while humming Maddie's Dance Party favorites. I danced in the shower. I danced while brushing my teeth. I danced while talking on the phone. I danced to channel Maddie. I danced to channel love. I danced to channel life. Because as Maddie showed me, I am better when I am dancing.

That mantra was on full display this evening. Post *Miffy the Movie*, I knew this was our last night before the Cancer gavel officially would fall. The Judgment of the fluid results awaited us early in the morning. But instead of mourning until morning, we took Maddie's lead. With me, Gaga, Pop Pop, and Aunts Jennifer and Jamie huddled around Maddie's Lurie's Place hospital bed, Maddie issued the following order:

"DANCE!"

It was like a command from above. In the form of our three-year-old hero. Maddie yet again leading us gracefully down the proper path through darkness. And so dance we did. All five of us, in all of our uncoordinated glory, following Maddie's direction. Armed with an iPhone and an unstoppable spirit, Maddie lifted us all up to the high heavens on a night when we were otherwise being driven down into the depths of hell. If she detected even a minor pause in our movements, Maddie roared back:

"KEEP DANCING!"

Better yet, as Meghan Trainor finally concluded the Maddie Dance Party playlist, my dance partner in crime looked up at me from the hospital bed. "Daddy, can I dance with you?" Up she went. Into my weary arms. Each of us holding one another with every ounce of energy remaining. Dancing away. Just like we've been doing since the day she was born.

Whatever happens tomorrow, I promise you this. Maddie will always be with us. And we will never stop dancing. Because of you, Maddie, we are — and will always be — better when we're dancing.

Miracles and Lights Revisited (12/20/17)

While lighting a *menorah*, you are to light each candle methodically from left to right. You do not move to the next candle until the preceding candle is fully lit. As I lit the *menorah* on Monday night (the night before we returned to Lurie's Place for the fluid tests), something subtle yet extraordinary happened. As expected, Candles 1 through 3 lit with ease. A brief touch of the lighter, and the candle glowed brightly. But when I approached Candle 4, the challenge escalated unexpectedly. No matter how many times I returned to the pesky wick, the candle refused to light. Touch after touch of the lighter, the candle resisted.

But I wasn't giving up. I couldn't give up. Pammy and I both stood in front of the resistant *menorah* knowing full well that these candles now represented our Miracles and Lights. We exchanged glances as if to share a feeling that Maddie's fate was somehow connected to these lousy candles. Real or not real, we weren't taking any chances. To watch them refuse to light before our eyes was not an option. So I kept at it. And oddly, the same pattern continued with each remaining candle. Candle 4, Candle 5, Candle 6, and Candle 7, each as difficult to light as the next. Refusing to give into the resistance, we concluded the seventh night of Hanukkah with seven brightly glowing lights. Our Miracles and our

Lights, despite a slightly longer path than anticipated, were on full display.

The symbolism was striking to me and Pammy. Although I had hoped to be able to write something about this extraordinary lighting earlier, Saturday brought our hopes of Miracles and Lights to a crushing halt. And our oncology team's concern with an even broader spread of cancer cells to Maddie's cerebrospinal fluid had Pammy and me both going to sleep last night, awaiting the fluid sample test results, feeling as if this fluid had drowned out any remaining Miracles and Lights left on our metaphorical A.C. *menorah.*

I should've known better when it comes to Maddie. Don't Stop Believin', right?

Because at 1:00 p.m. this Wednesday afternoon, at the absolute basement of this latest nightmare, Dr. Jason lit a new candle of hope and posited a pathway up to daylight. The result of the first fluid sample test? No cancer cells. You read that correctly – no signs of new cancer cells in Maddie's fluid in this first test. In light of certain ambiguities in the test, he wants to do one more test to be sure, but he is now optimistic that the fluid itself is clear. If true, that would mean there is nothing more comprehensively destructive going on inside Maddie's cerebrospinal fluid itself beyond the five-millimeter spot. Alternatively, if Maddie were to test positive for cancer cells in her fluid, then Hope would be removed from the A.C. Equation.

Instead, at least for tonight, we can continue to believe that Maddie just has a limited, albeit tremendously treacherous, medical problem. That she just has a recurrence of a lone tumor at the base of her previous site. While this alone would still be challenging news, Dr. Jason confirmed that we would still have an option. We would still have a Hail Mary at Hope (a fitting game plan given

Maddie's namesake, Mary). Although the doctors are continuing to finalize the specific plan of attack, there at least would be a plan. For now, we are able to hope. We are able to dream. We are able to continue to attempt to light those last few resistant cancer treatment candles even if the path is longer than anticipated. We are able to continue to believe in Miracles and Lights.

Quite a conclusion to the Hanukkah holiday. Welcome back, Miracles and Lights. Here's to seeing you shining brightly again next year. And to more favorable test results to come.

Maddie Medical Update (12/21/17)

Team Maddie,

It's been a rollercoaster of events and emotions since Saturday. More accurately, it's like someone took us, tossed us into a blender, and threw our mangled remains into a roller coaster on hyperdrive. But as we are discharged from Lurie's Place tonight, and look forward to the plan ahead, it at least feels like our actual bodies have returned to the front of the coaster, riding sturdy up to the next peak at the direction of our amazing medical team, even if we don't know what awaits at the end of this next upward stretch.

Here are the latest developments. First and foremost, we received results of a final test confirming that Maddie does not have free floating cancer cells in her cerebrospinal fluid at the moment. This is unbelievably miraculous news. Our doctors were concerned that Maddie's head pain may have been caused by an army of cells marching through her fluid, which would've marked a turning point in this A.C war that we pray never arrives. But instead, with no such cells present, we are all able to keep fighting. We are able to keep hoping. We are able to be the ones marching on.

This does not eliminate the concerns with the five-millimeter spot. However, we now understand that there are some characteristics suggesting the spot is a tumor, and there are other characteristics suggesting it is not. The doctors are extremely concerned (and the implications would be major), but they are not certain. With that in mind, the game plan is to schedule Maddie for surgery the week of New Years, so they can resect the spot and find out the truth. Beforehand, she'll have an MRI to confirm that the image hasn't changed in any meaningful way to suggest an alternate course.

There are a lot of what ifs based on what they find. But there are two main takeaways for which we are eternally grateful at this exact moment. One, the surgery itself is not as risk-laden as her April procedure. She won't have to wear a "necklace," and the recovery time expects to be much quicker. Two, assuming no other changes, even if the five millimeters are tumor, we will still be able to proceed with a new, albeit longer, treatment protocol.

And so with an exhausted, heavy, and hope-filled heart, I am thrilled to relay that our Miracles and Lights are still flowing with full force. Maddie is not done dancing. She is not done fighting. She is not done being Maddie.

Thank you all for the unparalleled outpouring of love and support. We are beyond blessed.

Maddie Medical Update (12/26/17)

Maddie turned three-and-a-half years old today. To celebrate, we experienced a day that felt like three-and-a-half years long, only to end with a miraculous gift greater than any birthday party could offer.

The morning began at 2:30 a.m. After five consecutive amazing nights at home, Maddie woke up complaining of head pain again. She proceeded to vomit at least five times over the course of the hour. Our holiday roller coaster ride was apparently not over. Despite the single digit temperatures outside, we bundle up and head straight to the Lurie's Place ER.

Déjà vu all over again.

They want to do another "quick" MRI to see if the ventricles in Maddie's brain are showing any new, emergent concerns. I assume, since we just went down this road last week, that it's just precautionary. A few hours later, I see a call on my cell phone from a private number. I pick up at my own risk.

In light of the holidays and the time of day, it's the oncologist dialing in remotely. I know immediately that means there's an issue. He goes on to explain that there's a new spot on Maddie's MRI but in a different location. Right at the base of Maddie's Ommaya Reservoir in her head. A spot that wasn't on the last MRI. The second concerning spot in ten days. More troubling, the location of this one potentially explains her previously undiagnosed headache and nausea symptoms.

So they order another more detailed MRI. Here we go again. In the past ten days, Maddie has been to the hospital three times, underwent four MRIs (two under anesthesia), and endured one CT scan. What does a girl have to do to just get a partridge in a pear tree around here?

The looks on all of the doctors faces today tell the story. Two spots in ten days. Inexplicable nausea and head pain. The coincidences seem too great. All signs point in one malignant direction. No one on the medical team is exactly emanating hope. The hours start to drag on again. It's past 5:15 p.m. and still no word on the MRI results. Pammy and I remember what this wait meant just a few days ago when the five-millimeter spot was revealed. We can't take it anymore. So we take it upon ourselves to walk down the hall, straight to the doctors' offices on the oncology floor, and meet our fate. We beg for an update.

"No tumor," she says softly.

And like that, our internal, emotional balloon of terror deflates. Cue the birthday balloons instead. Happy three-and-a-half-year-old birthday, Maddie. We won't be forgetting it any time soon. And the doctors won't be forgetting Maddie any time soon. As of now, they still can't explain the symptoms she's experiencing (although they are managed well by steroids). Their primary theories this week consistently revolved around new tumor (separate and apart from the five-millimeter spot), which would send us shooting down the rollercoaster at warp speed only for our now three-and-a-half-year-old hero to shoot down the theories and pull us up yet again. While we still do not know definitively what is causing Maddie's symptoms, for now, the previous game plan emerges from today unscathed. Surgery to be scheduled for next week (as the issue of the five-millimeter spot remains unresolved) and pray for more miracles to follow.

As today eventually came to a close, Aunt Jamie played a fitting tune. *I'm Still Standing,* the Taron Egerton version. A perfect song for a perfect girl. Maddie defying doctors yet again. She's still standing, alright. Donning a diaper with three visible words on her backside:

Born to Win.

I see a new Huggies model ready to roll. Or at the very least, I see the bravest person of any age (or any diaper size) who I have ever met. Happy Birthday, Maddie.

Maddie Medical Update (12/27/17)

Team Maddie,

We are all back at home again. Safe, sound, exhausted, and blessed. We regrouped with the doctors today before discharge. The next day consensus on Maddie's head pain and nausea is that there is no consensus. Only theories. All in all, despite the uncertainty, it's excellent news. We're just in one of those situations where uncertainty is a good thing. With ambiguity comes continued hope. For now, our oncologist feels comfortable that the diagnostic tests performed do not show any current signs of tumor or tumor cells in Maddie's brain or in the fluid around her brain.

As for next steps, Maddie is tentatively scheduled for surgery on January 2nd. She'll have an MRI that morning and, absent anything unexpected, proceed with surgery to remove and biopsy the five-millimeter spot from her spine. Whether or not that spot is tumor will dictate the steps that follow. In the meantime, however, we have narrowed the areas of imminent concern over the past two weeks. We pray to keep it that way between now and January 2nd.

Thank you all for your prayers and healing thoughts during this unimaginable time. Maddie continues to be the light that provides us the energy to keep moving forward. We are in awe of her each and every day. The level of sleep deprivation, disruption, and invasiveness she experienced this week – at just three-and-a-half years old – only to emerge as silly, happy, and innocent as ever, is as miraculous as it gets. We will rest easy tonight, in the comfort of our own beds, feeling grateful for Maddie and for all of the love and strength that has lifted up our family this week.

Just Keep Swimming (12/28/17)

In the six months B.C., Pammy, Maddie, and I spent every weekend going to swim class. If you haven't had the experience of a newborn or toddler swim class, it's definitely a must on the parent checklist. Putting aside the fact that getting your child dressed and undressed takes about 10 times longer than the 30-minute session itself, the time in the pool is just incredible.

Perhaps most remarkable is the bond you feel with your child in those moments. Especially as you're teaching them to actually go under water, hold their breath, and assist them back up. For parents who have experienced those brief, early, underwater moments, you know the feeling. I can picture myself telling Maddie to jump toward me, watch as she doggy paddles under water for a bit, struggling to stay afloat while learning to hold her breath, and the enormous physical and emotional exhale that comes when I pick her up with both hands and pull her above water for her first post-submersion breath. She smiles ear to ear, as she wipes away the water dripping down from her curly hair off her long eyelashes.

What an accomplishment. Taking the plunge. Trusting her Daddy to pick her up soon enough to avoid that drowning feeling. Emerging victorious.

But those brief seconds under water, especially early on in the learning process, are borderline terrifying. The only

252

saving grace in those moments is the fact that I know I'm in total control of the situation. I'm able to count the amount of time she's under water. I'm able to pluck her out safely before she falls deeper. I'm able to play the role of protector. Of lifeguard. Of Daddy. And the reward of that incomparable smile and deep breath is unparalleled.

And that's what we did every Saturday. We kept swimming. We kept going under. We kept coming back up.

In many ways, our time at swim class represents another life. The essence of life B.C. On a most basic level, it's one of the few activities that Maddie has been unable to replicate or continue in any way, shape, or form in her life A.C. Because of her central line, she's unable to be in the water. And those B.C. swimming memories are so pure, so fun, and so beautiful, that they sit as one of those nostalgic and difficult reminders of what once was.

But on a broader scale, swimming class represented the last time that we felt in full control of Maddie's fate. No longer do we have sole authority for whether and when Maddie is plucked from her underwater submersion. While we are both in the pool together in the A.C. World, at times it feels as if our hands are tied behind our backs. And we are just left to watch. And pray. As someone or something pulls Maddie farther away to the deep end of the pool.

The past two weeks have been an absolute gut-wrenching reminder as to the complete lack of control that comes with Cancer. The helplessness is horror. On three occasions this past week, Pammy and I have waited for results that would imminently dictate Maddie's fate. To determine whether she would emerge from her underwater plunge. And we were left powerless in those results.

As we wait for Maddie's next surgery, the lack of control is palpable. And the resulting pain is excruciating. The feeling alone is as close to drowning as I've ever experienced. Every time Maddie touches her neck, even if innocently, I feel myself struggling for breath. Every time the doctor's phone number shows up on my caller I.D., the helplessness thrusts into my throat.

In those moments, however, I focus on bringing myself back. Back to everything Maddie has taught me over the past 8 plus months. Back to everything we have been forced to learn in order to tread above water in the Cancer Pool. And I think in some ways the reminder comes back to this:

The only thing we don't control is the ultimate medical outcome.

I can't minimize the pain that comes with that reality. But I also can't dwell on it. I have to focus on what we continue to control. Because we continue to control the support we provide Maddie. We continue to control The Narrative, however fluid it must be, as well as the lens through which Maddie experiences this unthinkable journey. We continue to control the way we support one another. We continue to control our actions. Our words. Our love.

And in these otherwise helpless times, we must continue to exercise that control – perhaps more than ever – to help Maddie and each other stay afloat. We must keep swimming. We must keep swimming for the sake of Maddie. We must keep swimming for the sake of Lily. We must keep swimming for the sake of each other. We must keep swimming for the sake of life.

And so while I pray that the end of this story results in Maddie emerging from this cancerous pool and returning to her weekend extracurricular dips, I know this: No matter what, we will keep swimming.

Maddie Medical Update (12/30/17)

Team Maddie,

Our hope for a restful reprieve before January 2nd was not in the cards. Maddie woke up in the early hours this morning again complaining of escalating pain despite her medicinal regimen. And so for the third time in the past two weeks, we returned to the Lurie's Place ER only this time to be admitted promptly to the 17th Floor (Maddie's favorite floor) for pain management.

Although Maddie was excited for her upcoming sleepover as usual, her now stronger pain medicines have her sleeping continuously.

Please send your strongest prayers these next couple of days. We have a lot of unanswered questions as Maddie's surgery date grows closer. And her escalating symptoms have us all a bit worried while holding on to hope for positive developments.

Most importantly, however, the medications are managing her pain again. She is resting peacefully. As sweet and cute as ever.

A New Year's Lesson from Lily (12/31/17)

Lily is a Miracle and a Light. I cannot even begin to fathom the last 24 hours, or the 48 hours to come until surgery, without her brightness. This otherwise pitch-black point on the A.C. Timeline is our darkest hour since the clock struck midnight on April 21, 2017. With the New Year just hours away, Maddie is regressing rapidly. I'm hard pressed to put much detail into writing if only because I'd prefer never to remember this precise moment. Suffice it to say, no one should ever experience this type of struggle. Or even read about someone else's dive into this darkness.

But in some ways, as I look around the 17th Floor, it's also a reminder of how blessed we've been over the past year. Despite this destructive disease, and an aggressive chemotherapy regimen, save for a few passing moments before today, Maddie's light never stopped shining. To the point when, just a few days ago, as people would say, "May 2018 be a better year," I hesitated in my reaction. Because up until these last 24 hours, 2017 was an incredible year. Cancer did not define our year. Cancer did not define Maddie. Maddie defied Cancer. Maddie defined Maddie. And the Miracles and Lights that graced 2017 were something to celebrate and continue. Not something to warrant turning the calendar page.

That all changed yesterday. Pain has overtaken joy. Cancer has, for this moment, covered light. And we just pray for the strength to get to January 2nd irrespective of what that date will hold.

Enter Lily.

At just shy of 11 months of age, Lily is still a baby of few words. And few movements. Her primary dialect remains Smiling and Clapping. Yet her bubbly body language is just as full of expressiveness as any otherwise babbling baby.

In the ongoing juggling act of caring for Maddie and Lily in two different places, I spent a few hours in the afternoon yesterday with Lily Bug. Her light was infectious. As we made our way through lunch, books, dancing, and playtime, Lily managed to bring a joy otherwise being ripped out of us for the last 24 hours. For that and more, I am forever grateful to Lily. Her most recent 24 hours of light are just small examples of the solar power she's shined upon our family this year.

Lily's solar powered energy has also carried a curious, unexpected message. Over the past few weeks, Lily has been trying to muster the physical energy to crawl. Only for the time being, she's capable of going in just one direction:

Backward.

Try as she might, our cheeky cherub can't quite figure out forward progress. She's grunting, pulling, and pushing with all her might, but it is now abundantly clear that before she moves forward she is going to have to go backward.

Before she moves forward she is going to have to go backward.

And so as we get ready to turn the page on 2017, and as we crawl closer to Maddie's January 2nd surgery date, I am doing my best to channel Lily. To accept that sometimes backward must precede forward. I'll admit, I have no idea how far the backward slide we're currently on goes. The possibilities terrify me to my core. And while I also can't yet envision what forward might look like, I know that forward will come eventually. No matter what. Fueled by the same Miracles and Lights that powered this otherwise blessed year.

Maddie Medical Update (1/1/18)

Team Maddie,

We are especially grateful for all of your prayers in this new year. They were much needed over the course of the last 24 hours. Early this morning, Maddie's Ommaya Reservoir ballooned in size indicating a rapid change in her intracranial pressure. I just happened to notice the change in between our brief Lurie sleep cycles. At this moment, I'm not capable of re-describing the horrifying symptoms and events that followed. But I am happy to share our day's miracle.

Just as Maddie was brought to the ICU for surgery prep to relieve the pressure, our Super Doctor – Dr. Alden – unexpectedly returned to Lurie's Place after a brief Florida vacation. A welcome face after a weekend of holiday hospital skeleton crews. He is, and forever will be, one of our most sacred care providers. Maddie underwent emergency surgery under his trusted hands to install a device to empty what ultimately turned out to be excessive blood in the fluid surrounding her brain. On a positive note, we at least have an explanation for what was causing her headaches themselves. We now just don't know what is causing the underlying bleeding. One piece of the puzzle solved. The broader enigma remaining.

Until further notice, Maddie will remain in the ICU for monitoring. Thankfully, she is stable and coherent at the moment (with a few vintage Maddie moments we haven't experienced in days). Surgery will be postponed, as the doctors want to first further analyze and address her bleeding and the underlying cause. Maddie is scheduled for an MRI of her spine tomorrow, which should provide an update on the five-millimeter spot and all other things spinal.

After an utterly terrifying start to the new year, we go to sleep praying that Maddie will experience a few days of well-deserved calm. As always, but perhaps under more extreme circumstances than ever, she was a champion of strength today. Please keep the prayers coming. Thank you all for the constant love and support.

Maddie Medical Update (1/2/18)

Team Maddie,

We received Maddie's MRI results this morning. Although we finally have a likely answer to the past few weeks of pain and trauma, it's not the answer we have all been hoping to receive.

The five-millimeter spot grew significantly over the past three weeks. To the point where they believe this spot – now confirmed as tumor – is the primary cause of Maddie's pain (and possibly the mysterious bleeding as well). More concerning, there are two other spots on the MRI that are worrisome to the medical team.

Based on these findings, Dr. Alden proceeded today with the originally planned surgery to remove the former five-millimeter spot. The hope is that the surgery will help her bleeding and relieve Maddie's pain irrespective of what the ultimate game plan might be.

We've had a lot of information and emotions to digest over the past few days. As for immediate next steps, our medical team will be monitoring Maddie very closely, and we will re-evaluate as Maddie's symptoms evolve. For the time being, Pammy and I are just going to take this one day at a time. Our primary goal, no matter what, will be to keep Maddie as comfortable as possible. We will remain by

Maddie's side. We will stay strong. And we will give her every last drop of love and support within our bodies.

Uppa Daddy (1/3/18)

"Uppa, uppa," I can hear baby Maddie say. Her baby babble way to beg for me to pick her up. As Maddie gets a little older, she slowly enhances her word choice:

Afterward it's, "Uppa Daddy."

Then it's, "Wanna go Uppa Daddy."

Next it's, "Can I go Uppa Daddy?"

And finally it's now, "Daddy, can I come up?"

While all versions of the evolving Maddie ask for elevation are amazing, I always had a special place for "Uppa Daddy." Uppa Daddy usually came right before Maddie was ready to settle into The Nook for a nap or bed time. Or better yet, after the occasional pre-toddler meltdown, Maddie would calm herself down and surrender softly by saying, "Uppa Daddy." A sweet siren sound for snuggles. The request was always irresistible. And while, "Daddy, can I come up?" pulled quite hard at my Daddy heart strings in the last year or so, "Uppa Daddy" will always reign supreme.

At its core, Uppa Daddy is not just about physical consoling (although those snuggles never get old). Uppa Daddy represents something far greater. Uppa Daddy represents trust. Uppa Daddy represents security. Uppa Daddy represents love.

Trust. Security. Love.

Three critical components to any strong parent-child relationship. And Maddie was blessed with an outpouring of this TSL Trifecta from both her Mommy and Daddy. In both B.C. and A.C., our relationship with Maddie has been grounded firmly in TSL.

For the past 8 plus months, by continuing to build TSL, Pammy and I have waged a psychological and physical war against Cancer. With The Narrative, we built a Trust with Maddie that our words were gospel, and that her experience would match our simplified, toddler-friendly explanations of what was coming or happening in any individual A.C. moment. With our constant and warming presence, we ensured that Maddie always felt Security in her otherwise insecure surroundings. With our positive, empathetic, and supportive tone, we blanketed Maddie in unwavering Love. And with Maddie's bright light, and the support of family and friends, we were blessed with the endurance to keep providing Maddie with a steady dose of TSL, a triple threat more lethal to Cancer than any chemotherapy agent ever could be.

Unfortunately, the past few days have attempted to undermine the impact of TSL to the core. No matter how much we dial up the TSL, the aggressiveness of Cancer continues to overwhelm her physical body. But Pammy and I refuse to relent. Our Narrative – however many adjustments it may require – will not stop. Our constant and warming presence – no matter how many new settings this next phase surrounds us with – will remain ever-present. Our positive, empathetic, and supportive tone – despite all negative, cancerous pressures – will not back down.

As Cancer appears to be taking over, our only prayer is that Maddie can still find comfort in TSL. That ineffective medical interventions will not undermine Trust. That pain will not conquer Security. That palliative care will not replace our parental Love. And that we continue to have the strength to endure the unimaginable moments to come in order to maintain an ongoing infusion of TSL against an unforgiving force.

If I had any doubts, Maddie relieved those on New Year's Day following a 24-hour period that I would have otherwise preferred to erase from my mind. After experiencing intensive head pain, followed by her Ommaya Reservoir ballooning with fluid, followed by a "quick" brain MRI, followed by a seizure, followed by an emergency surgery to stop the bleeding in her brain, Maddie woke up to be transported for a CT scan. As always, we set the stage for Maddie. Based on preliminary explanations from the medical team, we told Maddie that she was going to take a "quick picture" so that we could try and "help her headaches go away" and that "nothing would hurt." Who knew how wrong we would be.

First, the I.V. team arrives promptly to advise that the dye for the CT scan cannot flow properly through Maddie's central line. So instead they have to place a new I.V. into Maddie's arm. So much for "nothing would hurt." Then we head downstairs for what is supposed to be a 5-minute scan. Upon arrival in the CT room, as the nurses begin to administer the dye, with Maddie lying horizontal in a virtual straightjacket, the I.V. line stops working. Maddie is forced to wait, in her same uncomfortable position, for more than 40 minutes as the I.V. team eventually returns, searches painfully for alternate veins, and eventually helps secure the line. 10 minutes later, the CT scan is complete. So much for "quick picture."

Nevertheless, Pammy and I willed Maddie through the entire prolonged and painful process. We brought an onslaught of TSL despite how grossly mistaken our initial instructions turned out. And when Maddie finally emerged from the scan, 45 minutes later than we promised, what did she do? Did she pout? Did she ignore us? Did she blame us for not telling her the truth (or at least, for our truthful instructions not coming to fruition)?

Nope. Not even close. Even when life didn't go to plan. Even when her quick and easy experience turned into a mini CT nightmare. Even in her discomfort. Maddie turned to the essence of TSL. And in her anesthesia-induced haze, she whispered two words. Two words that I haven't heard from Maddie's mouth in more than two years. Two words that define the TSL-driven strength of my relationship with Maddie.

"Uppa Daddy."

As Pammy and I lead Maddie down the next, treacherous lap of this A.C. journey, we do so knowing that the height of Maddie's TSL is at its lifelong peak. We've been cultivating her TSL day after day, hospital visit after hospital visit, and painful experience after painful experience. There is no doubt that what remains will be more difficult than anything we've experienced in our lives. But our job remains the same. TSL. We love you, sweet girl.

Maddie Medical Update (1/3/18)

Team Maddie,

As today wore on, Maddie's symptoms grew progressively worse. Her pain is rising rapidly in the precise location of the other spots on the MRI. The bleeding in her brain is not relenting. Cancer is not retreating.

After a day of tears and embraces, Maddie is transitioning into palliative care only. She is sleeping comfortably as we speak, and we are in the hands of an outstanding medical team. As always, Pammy and I are spending the evening by Maddie's side at Lurie's Place.

Of all rooms, we were placed on a new floor with a large Mickey Mouse decal directly outside of our window. There is literally no other room in the hospital with this view. We can't help but smile knowing that Mickey is by our side. His presence is a reminder of the cast of cartoon characters that joined Maddie on her heroic journey.

We will have difficult days ahead, but Pammy and I know that Maddie's story does not end here. And that the coming days will not in any way define her or the Miracle and Light she has been and always will be. Maddie has battled this wretched disease with an unparalleled grit and grace (and more than a few shimmy shakes). We are truly blessed to be by her side. And thankful for having such incredible support. We love you all.

Maddie Medical Update (1/5/18)

Team Maddie,

Maddie passed away peacefully last night at Lurie's Place. As you can imagine, we have a difficult time thinking of Maddie in those terms. We prefer to view her as dancing away, pain-free and happy as ever.

We promise you this, Maddie will always be with us. We will feel the warmth of her light, and the power of her miracles, as we move forward in life with her inspiration by our side.

Thank you all for the tremendous outpouring of love this week. Because of you, we have never felt alone during this entire journey. And that was never more apparent than the last few days. We are so appreciative for each of you.

Team Maddie Forever.

The New Beginning (Daddy's Eulogy) (1/7/18)

For many of us, today begins the same way as it did for me and Pammy on April 21st. With a lot of difficult questions. How could this kind of tragedy happen? Why should anyone ever have to experience this? How awful must it be to stand here as Pammy and I are forced to do today?

Here's my answer. Day in and day out, Pammy and I have refused to give in to that line of questioning. Since April 21st, we've created our own narrative. A narrative of love. A narrative of life. A narrative of light.

While no one should ever experience the brutality of cancer, everyone should have the beautiful blessing to experience Maddie. As we have all been fortunate to witness over the course of the past eight plus months, Maddie is an absolute Force. She is the force behind the narrative. A force of love. A force of life. A force of light. Maddie has taught us all more about life during this experience than most learn in a lifetime. She has left an impact on the people around her that is everlasting. She has shared her Miracles and Lights in a way that leave us all forever changed.

And so today I am not questioning how someone could be forced to stand here in my shoes. Instead, I am thinking about how filled with pride I am to stand before you. An unparalleled pride to be called "Daddy" by the most heroic human being I have ever met. And a pride for having a partnership with a wife who defies all adjectives. Pammy, what you have given to Maddie over her life is otherworldly. At some point along this journey, a good family friend sent me a text message. "Love is an action word," she wrote. You embodied that phrase. And watching you in action with Maddie was love at its finest. Your selflessness, your energy, your optimism, your dedication. Maddie is who she is because of you. Light begets Light. Love begets Love.

For me and Pammy, that begetting also most certainly extends to you as well. To Team Maddie. We are not standing here today, on our own two feet, without your boundless love and support. For those of you who have any doubt, remember that providing support to those facing hardship matters. You gave us the fuel to keep going. And despite the void we have in our lives, I feel so incredibly full right now looking out at this room full of all of you who helped us along the way.

I look at you, and I see our collective force of love – spanning from recent friends and longtime friends, family members, Maddie's gifted medical team (inpatient, outpatient, and home health), Lurie's Place family, PepsiCo family, Griffin McCarthy & Rice family, Sidley Austin family, University of Michigan family, University of Illinois family, Chicago Booth family, Camp Ramah family, and American Cancer Society family. What a blessing.

And what better representation of that collective force of love than the temple in which we're sitting. The home of Maddie's preschool, Gan Shalom. This synagogue has not just been a house of worship or a preschool to us. But a community. A community – led by the preschool director, the clergy, Maddie's teachers, and the fellow Yellow Room families – that embraced us and lifted us up on April 21st and haven't stopped carrying since. Leave it to the Yellow Room to be a bright and broad microcosm for the love and support we received from all of you.

I hope that over the next few weeks I will have the opportunity to thank so many of you individually for your specific acts of kindness. But for now, I do want to first thank my other roommate, Grandma Sue. Grandma, you should receive your Form W2 in the mail by January 31st. In all seriousness, you dropped your entire home life in New Jersey to bring into our home your endless supply of sweets, optimism, iPadding – and most importantly – your unquestionable love for Maddie and Lily. You did so at a time when we needed it most. Your help was the ultimate act of selfless love. Thank you, Grandma.

Gaga, Pop Pop, Grandpa, you all know the unbelievably special role you played in Maddie's life. She was just so blessed to be so loved by you all. To Maddie's Aunts, Uncles, and Cousins, we know how uniquely hard this is on you. But we are so grateful for the joy and energy you all brought to each and every visit, each and every imaginative play session, and each and every Maddie Dance Party. You were such a critical component of making this past year one of life and not one of struggle.

To each and every one of you, please know that we are forever grateful. We are all together and forever Team Maddie.

So where do we go from here? Or, as Maddie would say, "What's next?" My commitment today, to all of you, is that Maddie's story, and Maddie's life, will not be remembered as a tragedy. But as an inspiration. I ask you all – as a way to honor Maddie – to join us in that commitment. It's okay to feel upset right now. It's a necessary part of the grieving process. But let us also see the light of inspiration through the clouds of sadness. That's what Maddie deserves. That's how to honor Maddie. That's how to support our family. And that's our collective path forward.

Once we take our moments to mourn, Pammy, Lily, and I are dedicated to ensuring that the Miracles and Lights that Maddie has bestowed upon all of us are spread well beyond our family and friend circle. That Maddie continues to make her mark on the world around her. And that when we all channel Maddie, we don't just channel tears. We instead channel dancing. We channel singing. We channel imagination. We channel character playing. We channel strength. We channel love. We channel life.

I love you so much, Maddie. You will be with us wherever we go. Carrying us forward just as you always have. With a dance in our step, and a smile on our face.

Prologue Revisited (9/30/18)

Team Maddie,

As the publication date for *Maddie's Miracles* grew near, committing to a final chapter became increasingly difficult. To be honest, I struggled with including any ending to Maddie's story. Feeling as if her story should not conclude in any way, shape, or form. Because my prayer is that there is no conclusion to Maddie. That Maddie, her life, and her legacy shall instead transform into one giant love-filled ellipsis, which will dance on for eternity.

Although I attempted to ease the emotional burden by referring to the last chapter as "The New Beginning," the final chapter nonetheless memorialized the words I relayed at Maddie's funeral on January 4, 2018. But Maddie's story did not end on January 4th. Nor shall her beautiful Book of Life. Today, in honor of the ellipsis that will be Maddie's eternal literary light, we share this Prologue Revisited with endless love and appreciation.

For those who have been following our blog (http://maddiesmiracles.wordpress.com) since April 2017, or for those who are reading Maddie's story for the first time, the conclusion to Maddie's physical time here on this Earth came quickly. The unexpected, rapid conclusion to this Book of Life mirrored our all-too-rapid reality. But equally rapid was our commitment to ensure that Maddie's legacy was that of inspiration. To honor our promise to move forward with a dance in our step and a smile on our face.

And so this Prologue Revisited is very much a true new beginning. Because on this September 30, 2018, we announce the formation of our new lifelong, philanthropic commitment:

> Dancing While Cancering
> The Maddie Kramer Foundation

Formed in Maddie's honor, our 501(c)(3) nonprofit organization has one loving mission:

> *Bringing joy to the inpatient hospital experience for children with cancer.*

As promised, Pammy, Lily, and I are going to channel Maddie in the same ways that she inspired the world. In doing so, we are dedicated to helping existing and future patients battle cancer just as Maddie battled hers. Through dancing. Through singing. Through imagination. Through character playing. And through all the unbridled positivity that Maddie brought to her energetic, playful, and inspirational waltz across life's stage.

With the powers of love, life, and light, there are no endings. Only new beginnings. Thank you to Team Maddie, for continuing to give us the strength to keep going. And thank you to Maddie, our one in a million hero, for inspiring each and every step of our life's dance.

We love you, sweet girl…

Made in the USA
Columbia, SC
07 November 2018